Compan
Revised Comn

2. All Age Worsnip Year A

Already published

Companion to the Revised Common Lectionary
1: Intercessions

Julie M. Hulme

Companion to the Revised Common Lectionary

2. All Age Worship Year A

EPWORTH PRESS

0 7162 0522 X

First Published 1998
by Epworth Press
20 Ivatt Way
Peterborough, PE3 7PG

Typeset by Regent Typesetting, London
Printed and bound in Great Britain by
Biddles Ltd, Guildford and King's Lynn

Contents

This book is dedicated to the memory
of the
Revd D. Mary Holliday
(1923–1997)

Introduction

God is love.
God loves you – me – us.
Prayer is that openness of heart and mind which allows us to accept
  God's love for us and offer ourselves to it.
God is always present and always ready to meet with us.
We surrender to the glory of God as God yearns to be revealed
  through us and in all things.
In our surrender, we learn how to live within the love of God and
  be transformed by it.
  And God-in-us meets and transforms the world.

Prayer then is essentially very simple. And yet, because we are complex, multi-layered personalities, it is often very difficult to pray. Our bodies are tense, our emotions are unstable, our minds wander or are daunted by the scale of the world's pain – and in the depths of our souls we battle with a deep reluctance born of guilt and shame, anger and fear. In our fragmented state we are not conscious of any peace for ourselves, or any blessing for others. At such times, it is only by faith that we can continue in prayer at all.

All prayer is a receiving or an offering – or both. It is like answering the door. Getting to the door can be hard work in itself, but what follows is utterly beyond our control. For the knock at the door is the wild wind of the Spirit, the Lover and Stranger who desires not only communion with us, but our companionship on an unpredictable journey. And so we struggle with prayer not least because we are awed at what is asked of us.

This being so – how do we go about leading prayer in corporate worship? How dare we attempt it? We do so by remembering not our frailty but the One who is present to us in our praying. It is God's love and grace which make prayer possible: God's desire to meet us for communion, healing and joy; and our faith in that even when all else fails us.

God is the source and spring of our praying together. Any moment when we meet to pray is a space marked out for God's purposes. The beginning of an act of worship takes us over a threshold into the place of encounter. What follows happens at God's initiative. The 'life-giving' quality of worship does not lie in its content as such but in the extent to which those taking part yield the time and the content to God. Liturgy or free praise? Hymns or choruses? Written or extempore prayer? All these distinctions are, in the end, irrelevant. What matters is that whatever is offered is *offered*, that is, in the hearts of the worshippers surrendered to God.

For the preacher or leader of worship, there is a very strong temptation to keep hold, to retain control, to resist surrendering the offering because we are afraid of what will happen if we let it go. But the renewal of the Body of Christ begins with the humility with which we prepare worshippers for such a direct and transforming encounter, help them interpret what is going on, provide signposts guiding them through, and enable them later to step back into the narrative of their daily lives. The imagery, structure and rhythm of our verbal praying supplies this framework, assisted by the readings, hymns and other elements of the service. Yet the real prayer is what the congregation offers *within* this framework.

So the structure must be sufficient, without becoming an obstacle. Leading public prayer is a task to be undertaken with gentleness, as the outbreathing of a love so tender that it does not break a bruised reed or quench a flickering flame. As far as possible, we must not place ourselves between the people and their Lord. The words exist to stimulate a response, not to us, but *to God*, so imagination, creativity and risk must be submitted to our loving knowledge of the congregation with whom we pray.

On the other hand, we must avoid clichés, and that excessive caution which stifles the Spirit by defining too closely what an image should mean. Our knowledge of Christian theology is the foundation of our praying, not its *life*. Prayer is always pushing at the limits of words because God is not only in our words but beyond them, and we are bringing each other to the point of surrender into that unknown.

Our corporate praying has to be built around what at first seems to be an empty space. We do not *fill* this silence with words: rather, we *create* it with word-structures, word-pictures, spoken, sung or chanted rhythms, and with story. This space is larger than the words themselves and reaches into an infinity which is within, between and yet beyond us.

All our verbal or written prayers are working towards that moment when together we step off the edge into the abyss which is the wordless, soundless, endless love of God in Christ. Once we have made that step, we are no longer in control. But we are surrendered to the love which holds us, feeds us, heals us, renews us; and sends us out as seeds of fire to light the world.

Julie M. Hulme
February 1998

Using this book

The readings on which this book is based are from the Revised Common Lectionary Year A, as adapted for use by preachers in the Methodist Church, but as great care has been taken to draw out major images and themes in the material, I hope that it will be useful to those who are following other lectionaries, as well as those who order their worship in other ways.

An authorized lectionary is, in one sense, an embodiment of the church's response to the Word of God. It is one way in which the ancient and universal church speaks to the local congregation, passing on what it has 'received from the Lord'. The Revised Common Lectionary contains a vast amount of material, including numerous 'optional' readings. While remaining faithful to the seasons of the Christian year, the Lectionary also provides great scope for those preachers and congregations who wish to read scripture in sequence. In editing and writing this book, I have tried to provide preachers with a flexible and practical tool which will give them a door into this embarrassment of riches and which will go some way towards reconciling the needs of those who prefer sequential readings, and those who prefer a 'thematic' approach.

In doing so, I have had to simplify the material in a number of ways. For example, the Lectionary contains readings for both morning and evening: the readings quoted in this book are drawn from the morning only. Over Christmas, and in Holy Week, the full lectionary includes a much wider range of readings than those listed here. Selecting is subjective and restrictive, but I have tried to offset this with an extensive thematic index and suggestions for prayers which might be used on festivals which are not covered in detail (see Appendix 3).

There is a section for each Sunday of the year, plus the major Christian festivals which fall mid-week, reflecting the growing importance of mid-week worship. The titles and themes are suggestions for those preachers who need an 'entry point' into the material, but the prayers relate to the readings themselves, not just to the theme. The suggestions for illustrating the theme are not fully worked through in terms of presentation and often consist of a series of questions. They are intended to give an idea of how the diverse nuances of the readings might be brought together into a coherent whole, and what issues arising from the text might need to be addressed. An attempt has been made to provide a strong visual theme for each week.

These prayers have been written for use with people of all ages, which means that, generally speaking, the construction, language and thought-forms have been kept fairly simple without avoiding 'long words' altogether. There is a strong emphasis on symbols and imagery, on congregational responses and on the use of rhythm and repetition. Although, following the practice of Jesus, God is still addressed as 'Father', other forms of address are explored, including some which respect the feminine in the divine. The imagery of light has been retained, but the 'light = good, dark = evil' dichotomy has been avoided wherever possible.

For any given Sunday, the book probably contains more material than can be used in a particular service: the aim has been to pay attention to the different elements of prayer and give the preacher maximum choice in how they should be put together. In combining elements, such as Adoration-Confession-Thanksgiving it is worth reflecting on how the space between the prayers might be used – the insertion of silence or music at these points can enhance the whole. Although each prayer stands alone, most of them have been written so that they can be used together in this way – and not just those where this is indicated in the text. It is for this reason that concluding phrases such as 'through Jesus Christ our Lord' have been omitted.

Suggestions are given in each section for a Call to Worship, but to be fair, they do not all contain the element of 'call', some being rather a thematic introduction or heading. Prayers of Adoration, Confession and Thanksgiving follow. Sometimes the element of penitence is served by a Prayer of Acknowledgment which is less to do with individual confession and more concerned with our general awareness of the pain and evil present in our community and the world. Declarations of Forgiveness are implicit in some prayers, and some of the Prayers of Thanksgiving can be used in this way, but where a more specific declaration is needed, suggestions can be found in Appendix 1.

Similarly, prayers relating the seasonal readings to Communion have been included in Appendix 2, in order to reflect not just the growing importance of the Eucharist in Sunday and midweek worship, but also the trend towards including children in the celebration.

Prayers of Intercession are not included, as these are the subject of the first book in this series, but many of the Prayers of Petition could be used as part of intercessory prayers if required.

The Prayers of Dedication have been written to fulfil a variety of needs: they can be used after Confession, or as a response to the Word, or to conclude prayers of intercession, or at the dedication of the offering. The Prayers of Dismissal serve not only to bless the departing congregation but also commission it for service in the world. There are a number of Meditations scattered throughout the book, some of which are more complex in form, and repay careful reading.

Contributors

I am grateful to a number of contributors who have collaborated with me in writing prayers or in supplying ideas which I developed. The numbers indicate the prayers for which they should receive credit:

DAVID BAGWELL is a Methodist minister whose responsibilities include a 'church plant' – joint Anglican–Methodist LEP involving regular all-age worship with 'unchurched' families. 241, 243, 245, 250, 251, 252, 255, 256, 257,258, 263, 264, 265, 268, 269, 270, 431, 432, 438.

PATRICIA BATSTONE was accredited as a Methodist local preacher in 1964. She is a freelance writer, poet and editor with experience in teaching and bookselling. 113, 117, 120, 121, 123, 124, 125, 126, 127, 129, 130, 131, 133, 135, 136, 137, 138, 140, 141, 143, 144.

STEVEN BROWNING is a Methodist minister and university chaplain. He has experience of an Anglican–Methodist 'church plant' and a keen interest in the development of community liturgy. 332, 334, 338, 339, 344, 349, 355, 441, 442.

TIM CROME is a Methodist minister with extensive experience of work on housing estates with 'inner city' problems. His current responsibilities include an Anglican-Methodist congregation which meets in a community centre. He has served as chaplain to The Queen's College, Birmingham. 304, 305,307, 309, 311, 312, 315, 316, 317, 318, 319, 321, 322, 323,324, 327, 328, 329, 434, 436.

ALBERT GAYLE is a Methodist minister with experience of prison chaplaincy and work in schools. He is a member of the Ordinands' Retreat Leadership team. 273, 274, 275, 276, 277, 278, 279, 283, 284, 285, 291, 292, 294, 295, 297, 298, 300, 301, 424.

PAULINE GREASLEY is a primary school teacher and a Methodist local preacher, with interests in meditative prayer and creative worship for all ages. 1, 2, 4, 9, 11, 14, 16, 19, 21, 22, 24, 32, 34, 35, 38, 421, 422.

JANE LEACH is a Methodist minister with experience in midweek clubs for 'unchurched' children and work within schools. She enjoys working with families to develop accessible liturgies for baptisms,weddings and funerals. 185, 187,1]89, 191, 193, 194, 196, 198, 199, 200, 202, 204, 206, 209, 210, 212.

ALISON PEPPER currently works as a secretary and is the organist at her local Methodist church. With a background in theology, she has a growing interest in writing prayers and meditations which link personal experience with the worship of the local community. 49, 50, 52, 64, 72, 429.

FIRST SUNDAY OF ADVENT

Isaiah 2.1–5; Psalm 122; Romans 13.11–14; Matthew 24.36–44

AWAKENING TO LIGHT

Presentation

Illustration: an alarm clock. Do we find it easy to wake up in the morning? Or to stay awake when we need to be bright and alert? What do we use to help us? What do we miss – in creation, and in other people – if we are too dull or self-centred to look around us? Are we in danger of missing the new thing God is doing in the world?

(1) Call to Worship

Isaiah 2.2–3a, Psalm 122.1; *or the following:*
Read Romans 13. 11–12

Wake up! Wake up! **The light of a new dawn breaks.**
Get up! Get up! **Meet the light of the morning.**
Come, come now! **To meet the Lord of light on his earthward
  way.**

(2) Meditation

It has been night: now the sun rises,
bringing warmth and colour to the earth.
You are God: Creator and Lord of light,
bringing warmth and colour to our lives.
To all the world you give the promise of returning day:
to all the world you give the rainbow hope:
joy in orange, hope in green, peace in blue and love in red.
From the new brightness of Spring to the yellow ripening of
  Summer;
from the brown decay of Autumn, to the white sleep of Winter,
you are the beginning and the end, the everlasting God of hope,
life to all creation. May your name be praised in light!

*This meditation could also be used as an act of thanksgiving,
following prayers of confession.*

(3) Prayer of Adoration

Lord, we enter your house of beauty,
to discover life and joy in your presence:
for the night is drawing to its close:
And the day is almost here.

Lord, we enter your house of peace,
to deepen our communion with each other:
for the night is drawing to its close:
And the day is almost here.

Lord, we enter your house of justice,
where all that is wrong will be found out:
for the night is drawing to its close:
And the day is almost here.

Lord, we enter your house of learning,
where the Spirit will lead us into all truth:
for the night is drawing to its close:
And the day is almost here.

Lord, we enter your house of love,
where with people from all lands, nations, cultures and tongues,
we can join with the saints who have gone before us
as one great congregation, gathered in praise:
for the night is drawing to its close:
And the day is almost here.

(4) Prayer of Confession

Living, loving, forgiving God, we are sorry for sleeping so long:
for our morning stupor that leaves us neither awake nor aware.
Lord, forgive our sleepiness, our sluggishness of mind.
Silence.

We are sorry for not being ready: that we were not prepared for you,
not expecting to meet you, here, or in other people's needs.
Lord, forgive our lateness and our lack of preparation.
Silence.

We are sorry for not being there when you called us to work for you:
to help, to listen, to love and to pray.
Lord, forgive our absence and our failure to respond.
Silence.

We are sorry we have not paid attention: we have been too easily
distracted, too busy with our own affairs.
Lord, forgive our selfishness and our lack of care.
Silence.

We come in all humility to ask for your forgiveness:
Help us now to wake up, keep watch, and prepare your way.

(5) Prayer of Dedication

We praise you, God of unity,
for through the breadth and depth of your forgiveness,
we are reconciled to each other and to you.
Let us praise the God of love:
Come, let us walk in the light of the Lord.

We praise you, God of truth,
for you help us to see what is wrong, and put it right,
and you are at our side as we establish justice between individuals,
peoples and nations.
Let us praise the God of love:
Come, let us walk in the light of the Lord.

We praise you, God of peace,
for you strengthen all those who live compassionately
in the midst of hatred, and who teach others to make peace.
Let us praise the God of love:
Come, let us walk in the light of the Lord.

(6) Prayer of Dismissal

Go out in faith, bearing the armour of light
for the cause of God's peace,
as people of love and truth and praise.

SECOND SUNDAY OF ADVENT

Isaiah 11.1–10; Psalm 72.1–7. 18–19; Romans 15.4–13; Matthew 3.1–12

PRUNED BY LOVE

Presentation
Illustration: pruning shears/drawing of a shaggy 'bush' with a main stem and many unnecessary branches, deadheads and leaves. Discuss: why do we prune roses, and fruiting plants and trees? To produce more and better fruit. List together: what faults and wrongs did the prophets wish to see 'pruned' out of the people? What needs to be pruned from our own lives? Consider how this is done by repentance, and obedience to the word of God. What fruit might we then expect to see?

(7) Call to Worship

Isaiah 11.1–3 *or* Psalm 72.18–19.

(8) Prayer of Adoration

O God of all life, you call us to a life of praise,
so that we may share your word of joy:
O God of life, we praise your holy name.

O God of all truth, you call us to a life of purity,
so that in our homes, our work, and our communities,
your word of holiness can bear fruit in justice:
O God of truth, we praise your holy name.

O God of love, you call us to a life of dedication,
so that at all times, and in all places,
your word of hope may be recognized and your glory praised:
O God of love, we praise your holy name.

(9) Prayer of Confession

Father, Gardener of all creation, we are your fruit trees.
Our yield is poor, so you come to prune away our dead wood.
And we are afraid
    of the pain; of open wounds; of infection;
    of new growth which will change our shape, stimulate new
        shoots, and make us bend with the weight of fruit.
We are afraid that your pruning will make us different.
We have been dormant too long
    satisfied with ourselves, maintaining the cycle of life,
        but not being productive.
Forgive us, Lord, and prune away our complacency.
Prune away our pride. Prune away . . . (*other faults can be added from your list*)
Silence.

Now you are making us into new trees; trees that will feel the light on their leaves, draw the rain through their roots, and be nourished by the Gardener's care. May we blossom and bear fruit for you.

(10) Prayer of Thanksgiving

Loving Jesus, Word of God, we thank you

- for becoming a child, so that we would see how vulnerable God could be;
- for teaching of love, so that we could learn of God's promise to us;
- for acting in mercy, so that we could be healed through faith and prayer;
- for being obedient even to death, so that we could be saved to the uttermost.

Loving Jesus, Word of God, we thank you for your life of humble love in our midst, and for the example of those who have followed you in every age. Encourage us in their hope. Unite us with them in your praise.

(11) Prayer of Petition

Judge eternal, Lord of mercy, Father of us all:
your children are crying in pain and despair.
Because of our greed, they cry out for food:
Let your children be fed.
Because of our hatreds, they cry out for peace:
Let your children have life.
Because of our oppression, they cry out for justice:
Let your children be free.
Because of our apathy, they cry out for tenderness:
Let your children sing for joy.
Judge eternal, look upon us with compassion.
Lord of mercy, heal the wounds of the world.
Father of us all, reach out to the cold, the hungry and the lost:
Your kingdom come.

Silence, then read Isaiah 11.1–10.
This is the word of the Lord: **Thanks be to God.**

(12) Prayer of Dedication

O God of love, in obedience to your Word,
may we welcome one another as Christ has welcomed us:
That your mercy may be praised throughout the earth.
May we serve one another as Christ has served us:
That your mercy may be praised throughout the earth.
May we reveal your truth and confirm the promises you have made:
That your mercy may be praised throughout the earth.
May we learn more of your steadfast compassion for all people:
That your mercy may be praised throughout the earth.
May we encourage each other, so that we are all built up in hope:
That your mercy may be praised throughout the earth.
May we live together in harmony, and give glory to you:
That your mercy may be praised throughout the earth.

(13) Prayer of Dismissal

Read Romans 15.5–6.   Glory to God! **Glory to God!**
Read Romans 15.13.   Glory to God! **Glory to God!**

THIRD SUNDAY OF ADVENT

Isaiah 35.1–10; Psalm 146.5–10; James 5.7–10; Matthew 11.2–11

PREPARING THE WAY

Presentation

Illustration:'Roadworks' signs, spades, wheelbarrow, bucket, models of bulldozers etc. Why do we need people to repair the road – even if we don't use cars? What are the difficulties and hazards of a bad road? And the advantages of a good one? If well-built and well-repaired roads are necessary for safe travel and good communications, what does it mean for us to 'prepare the highway' for God?

(14) Call to Worship

Isaiah 35.3–4 *or* Psalm146.1–2, 10; *or the following:*

Prepare the way for the Lord!
Make straight paths for him!
Every valley shall be raised up;
Every mountain and hill made low;
the rough ground shall become level,
And the rugged places a plain.
The glory of the Lord will be revealed.
Prepare the way!

(15) Prayer of Adoration

O God of deliverance, we adore you.
Your life brings gladness and rejoicing, blossoming and abundance.
In your life we find our joy: we would live to your glory.
God, keep us in your holy way: **That we may sing your praise.**

O God of freedom, we adore you.
Your presence strengthens, encourages and saves.
In your presence we are recognized and valued:
we would live to your glory.
God, keep us in your holy way: **That we may sing your praise.**

O God of hope, we adore you.
You are bringing all creation to healing and fulfilment.
Your Spirit refreshes the arid places of our world,
and makes the deserts into fruitful gardens.
God, keep us in your holy way: **That we may sing your praise.**

(16) Prayer of Confession

Loving Father, we are ashamed.
We know that you have heard us moaning and grumbling about
other people. We confess that we have been cruel and unfeeling.
Father forgive us: **Renew your loving spirit within us.**

Loving Father, we are ashamed.
We have been impatient with others, not letting them fulfil tasks in
their own time by their own ability. We have undermined their
self-assurance and been arrogant in our own achievements.
Father, forgive us: **Renew your loving spirit within us.**

Loving Father, we are ashamed.
We have not encouraged others as we should. We have ignored
their efforts and not given praise where it was due. We have been
jealous of other peoples' achievements instead of rejoicing with
them.
Father, forgive us: **Renew your loving spirit within us.**

Loving Father, may we carry the life of Christ
in affirming words and kindly deeds;
sharing your confidence and trust in us,
and helping each other to travel in hope
towards the coming of your kingdom.

(17) Prayer of Thanksgiving

Read James 5.7–10.
Lord, for the patience which comes from gratitude,
receiving the seed of your word in our hearts,
and the watering of your Spirit as it grows:
We give you thanks and praise.

For the strength which comes through waiting,
discerning your gentle presence in our midst
and recognizing your Spirit at work
in humble ways among us:
We give you thanks and praise.

For the peace which grows from compassion,
as we bear with each others' frailties
and endure the harassment of the world:
We give you thanks and praise.

(18) Prayer of Dedication

Lord, may we learn to see your kindness
in breaking bread with the hungry, in preaching the good news,
in bringing joy to the poor, and in setting prisoners free.
Lord, let us see with your eyes.

Lord, may we seek your Kingdom
in lifting up those who are burdened,
in offering a refuge for the stranger,
in standing with those who are powerless
and in pleading for the condemned.
Lord, let us love with your heart.

Lord, may we honour your glory
in giving sight to the blind, in making the deaf to hear,
in healing the diseased, and in raising the dead.
Lord, let us work with your hands.

(19) Meditation

Expected Lord – We do not wear camel-hair coats. We do not eat
wild honey and locusts. We do not preach in the wilderness. But as
John the Baptist prepared the way for you, so we make our
preparations.

We do not have his charisma. We do not have strong words. We do
not argue people into repentance. But as he prepared other people, so
we too must help others to prepare themselves for your arrival.
Preparation at this time usually means parcels and presents, but
preparation for you, Lord, needs to be in prayer and praise.

Preparation at this time usually means food and festivities, but
preparation for you, Lord, requires forgiveness.

Preparation at this time usually means crackers and cake, but
preparation for you Lord, demands that we listen to you, so that we
may know you when you come to us in Spirit and in fire.

(20) Prayer of Dismissal

Go into the world to tell others what you have heard and seen in
    Jesus.
Go into the world to share his healing, liberating love.

FOURTH SUNDAY OF ADVENT

Isaiah 7.10–16; Psalm 80.1–7, 17–19; Romans 1.1–7;
Matthew 1.18–25

CONCENTRATED COMPASSION

Presentation

Illustration: concentrated washing powder, high-powered batteries, lenses. Adverts convince us that concentrated products have more power in the same (or less) volume. All that is unnecessary has been removed, and the power is focussed in a smaller space. Discuss how sunlight, focussed through a magnifying glass, will burn paper, or the way in which lenses magnify the lamp of a light-house. Can these illustrations help us to understand how the love of God might be focussed or concentrated in Jesus? But God's power is only effective if it is received, accepted, offered, dedicated. This is the way of obedience, as walked by Joseph and Mary.

(21) Call to Worship

Isaiah 7.14; *or the following:*

Read Matthew 1.23.
God knows our human nature, our frailness and our vulnerability.
God was made human in Jesus.
Jesus knows our pain, he knows our joy.
God who became human is with us now.
Let us worship and praise the Lord our God.

(22) Prayer of Adoration

'*Our God contracted to a span,
incomprehensibly made man.*' (Charles Wesley)

What wonder is in these words, Lord!
That you, God of all creation – sun, moon, stars and planets –
come to us as a vulnerable baby!
We stand in awe at the possibility of such an event.
We kneel in humility at such an act of giving.
It is beyond our understanding, Lord!

We have seen the adverts:
- a glass and a half of milk into one small chocolate bar
- double the amount of washes with a small box of powder
- the same size battery making the toy run twice as far.
Yet you did something far, far, greater –
arriving in our midst as a newborn child!
All that love so minutely concentrated.
Your love for all humanity as a single person.
You risked all on that astounding task;
you gave us everything you had to give.
We cannot find the words to express our wonder, our thanks, and
our praise. How great you are, Lord; how great you are . . .

(23) Prayer of Confession and Thanksgiving

Forgive us, God of steadfast love, that so often we refuse to see
you at work in ourselves, each other, and the world around us:
- for the sceptical attitudes which will not let us see your signs of
  hope
- for the prejudice which will not let us read your word of life
- for the obstacles which we place in the way of your healing
  power
- for the small-mindedness which restricts the flow of your grace.
Silence.
The Lord hears our prayer: **Thanks be to God.**

Thank you, God of steadfast love, that we can wait for your arrival
in our midst:
- in gestures of caring and in words of encouragement
- in touches of gentleness and in smiles of relief
- in the lightening of burdens and in each tender embrace
- in shouts of laughter and in songs of joy.
Silence.
The Lord hears our prayer: **Thanks be to God.**

(24) Prayer of Dedication

Read Matthew 1.18–25.
Lord, you chose Mary.
You asked her to bear a child for you.
She was afraid, but she said yes. Yes – to your future.
She could not weigh all the consequences,
but she gave herself to your bidding.
Lord, make us strong to say 'yes' to your future for us.

Lord, you chose Joseph.
You met him in a dream and told him of your plans.
He was afraid, but he said yes. Yes – to your dream.
He did not know everything that would happen,
but he obeyed your word and accepted responsibility for your Son.
Lord, make us humble enough to obey you.

Lord, in choosing Mary and Joseph, you chose us.
You ask us to bear your grace, and to accept the task of caring.
You want us to carry the life of Jesus within us, and to make it our
duty to love.
Lord, carry us beyond our fears.

Lord, your trust in us is overwhelming.
We are frightened by the responsibility – we cannot respond straight
away. We ask questions: what will this mean? Where will I go? What
will I do?
**Lord, Mary and Joseph said 'yes' for us. Help us to join our
'yes' to theirs.**

(25) Prayer of Petition or Dismissal

Living God, we call upon your love
as light to penetrate the unease, deceit and cruelty of the world.
In all places of shame: **Let your glory shine.**
In all homes of misery: **Let your glory shine.**
In all realms of hunger: **Let your glory shine.**
Wherever there is need or pain or suffering, let the concentrated
compassion of your grace bring renewal and hope: **Let your glory
shine!**

CHRISTMAS DAY

Isaiah 52.7–10; Psalm 98; Hebrews 1.1–4 (5–12); John 1.1–14

GOOD NEWS!

Presentation

Illustration: items associated with the celebration of good news: decorations, cards, invitation, flowers, cake, candles, songs etc. Discuss: how do we feel when we are carrying good news? What do we do to communicate it, share it, celebrate it? What are the similarities – or differences – between this and the way we celebrate Christmas? What is the 'good news' of Christmas that we want to communicate, celebrate and share?

(26) Call to Worship

Psalm 98.1–3 *or* 4–6; *or* Isaiah 9.2, 6–7.

(27) Prayer of Adoration and Thanksgiving

Gather items of good news or causes for celebration from among the congregation. These can be inserted into the prayer, or the prayer can stand as a summary of the list. A candle could be lit for every thanksgiving.

O God of all joy, we give you thanks and praise, for you have created the world, given us life, and provided for all our needs.
O sing to the Lord a new song: **For he has done marvellous things!**

For you have given us endurance in times of suffering, and courage in all our distress . . .
O sing to the Lord a new song: **For he has done marvellous things!**

For you have refreshed us when we grew weary, and given us peace in the midst of trouble . . .
O sing to the Lord a new song: **For he has done marvellous things!**

For you have brought us comfort when we were sorrowful, and consoled us in our grieving . . .
O sing to the Lord a new song: **For he has done marvellous things!**

For you have healed us when we were sick, revived us when we were discouraged, and renewed us when we were downhearted . . .
O sing to the Lord a new song: **For he has done marvellous things!**

For you have given us new life in Christ, that as he is born into the world, we can know new hope, new faith, new joy . . .
O sing to the Lord a new song: **For he has done marvellous things!**

(28) Prayer of Affirmation

Can be used after a silent or extempore confession or intercession.

Lord Jesus, you are the light there in the beginning, bringing all things into life, and giving knowledge and wisdom to all people.
You are our light: **And the darkness cannot overcome you.**

Lord Jesus, you are the light coming into the world, looking for those who will believe, who are ready to be changed into children of God.
You are our light: **And the darkness cannot overcome you.**

Lord Jesus, you are the light coming to us, and we receive you with open, trembling hands, wondering at your grace, marvelling at your glory.
You are our light: **And the darkness cannot overcome you.**

(29) Prayer of Petition or Dedication

God of all goodness and love,
as your Son Jesus Christ has appeared among us in grace,
offering himself into our life and death in the greatest mercy;
may we offer ourselves into the joys and sorrows of others,
as kindness, as healing, as hope.

God of all riches and majesty,
as your Son Jesus Christ received the gifts of strangers,
taking his place among those who knew their need of others;
may we learn the generosity of gratitude,
and so encourage the growth of talents for the blessing of all.

God of all wisdom and wonder,
as your Son Jesus Christ was heralded by visions and dreams,
revealed by signs in heaven and the songs of angels:
may we so radiate glad and tender zeal
that we may spread your joyous peace in word and deed.

(30) Prayer of Dedication or Dismissal

Go into the light, taking bread to feed the hungry, peace to heal
those who are wounded, and hope to renew those bowed down by
doubt or despair:
Living God, lead us from light into light.

Go into the light, taking encouragement to those in difficulty,
compassion to comfort those who grieve, and joy to share with the
lonely:
Living God, lead us from light into light.

Go into the light, as bringers of good news, as bearers of grace, as
those who carry mercy, and as witnesses to God's glory:
Living God, lead us from light into light.

(31) Prayer of Dismissal

Let us go into the day to celebrate God-with-us.
Let us go together to share God's mercy with all people.
Let us go in peace to live in God's joy.

FIRST SUNDAY OF CHRISTMAS

Isaiah 63.7–9; Psalm 148; Hebrews 2.10–18; Matthew 2.13–23

GOOD NEWS?

Presentation

Illustration: shadows. Demonstrate with a torch or lamp the way that strong light creates shadows. Discuss: what is the 'shadow side' of Christmas? – the uncertainty over lodgings, the pain of birth, the dirt of the stable, the murder of innocent children. We celebrate God-with-us in both the light and the shade, though the shadows leave us with uncomfortable questions.

(32) Call to Worship

Psalm 148.1–2, 13 *or* Isaiah 63.7; *or the following:*

The promise has been kept.
A new hope is given.
The Son of God is born.
We are here to greet him with wonder and with joy.
Let us praise and worship the living God revealed in human form.

(33) Prayer of Adoration

O God of creation, for you and through you all things exist.
　　You love us and know our needs: **We adore you.**
O God of all people, you have revealed yourself to us as Father and
　　friend. You love us and know our needs: **We adore you.**
O God of grace, yours is an abundant and bountiful grace, ever
　　flowing for our nourishment, nurture and care. You love us and
　　know our needs: **We adore you.**
O God of tomorrow, in your saving presence we find our freedom;
　　in your tenderness we find our strength; in your promise we
　　place our trust, now and forever.

(34) Meditation

The four readers start out as newspaper sellers, standing apart, who then begin to reflect together on the news they are advertising.

Voice 1: Read all about it! Mystery. Suspense. Murder!

Voice 2: Read all about it! The Son of God, born in a stable!

Voice 3: Read all about it! Narrow escape from massacre!

Voice 4: Read all about it! Herod murders the children!

Voice 1: Read all about it! It's a gripping story!

Voice 2: What a mystery – where did the baby Jesus come from?

Voice 3: What suspense – where can she have the baby? Will they get away? Where can they go?

Voice 4: Put like that it hardly sounds true – like something out of a novel, or Hollywood, or a thriller on TV.

Voice 1: Or just an everyday news story!

Voice 2: But it happened! The mighty God – all that mystery – made known to us in a baby!

Voice 3: The secret God, who keeps us waiting – is now born! The living God of new life escapes from death.

Voice 4: But the others didn't. The innocents never do.

Voice 1: Yes, we know. But just listen to the wonder of it! We read about it in the Gospels, we celebrate it every December, we say it in the Creed . . .

Voice 2: It's not a fairytale.

Voice 3: It happened.

Voice 4: So you say.

Voice 1: I know it sounds fantastic, unbelievable, out of this world. But we know it's true! It happened for us!

Voice 2: Marvel at the miracle of it.

Voice 3: What a blessing! Can't we just kneel in awe and wonder?

Voice 4: You mean like the people in the stable. In all that muck?

Voice 1: For him? Yes! For Jesus Christ. (*kneels*)

Voice 2: For the Saviour of the World. The Mighty God. (*kneels*)

Voice 3: Wonderful Counsellor. Everlasting Father. (*kneels*)

Voice 4: Not for them – but for the Prince of Peace. (*kneels*)

(35) Prayer of Confession and Acknowledgment

Hold us, God of hope, as we confess to you the sin and shame in our lives, and the sin and shame of the world of which we are part.
Silence.

Encourage us, God of mercy, as we ask your blessing on those relationships which we know fall short of your high love.
Silence.

Guide us, God of wisdom, as we seek to know the right, and the courage to establish your holiness in our homes and our communities.
Silence.

(36) Prayer of Thanksgiving

Caring God, as you have created all children for joy, we give you thanks for the children in our midst, and the children we carry in our hearts.
Merciful Jesus, as you blessed marriage and family life, we give you thanks for our relationships of love and friendship.
Living Spirit, as you lead us through sorrow to praise, we give you thanks for that grace which grants peace even in the midst of suffering, and which transforms our fear into trust and hope.

(37) Prayer of Petition

For those who run from threat or fighting, hunger or abuse:
Lord, be a sheltering hand.
For those who cannot run, who are in danger themselves and those they love:
Lord, be a guarding hand.
For those who, are not protected, and who are broken in body, mind, heart or soul:
Lord be a healing hand.
Where we can offer help to those in need or want or fear:
Lord be a strengthening hand.
That right may prevail, the weak be protected and the wicked brought to account:
Lord be a mighty hand.

(38) Prayer of Dismissal

Jesus has come into the world to give us faith.
We will carry the faith with us.
Jesus has come into the world to give us hope.
We will carry the hope with us.
Jesus has come into the world to give us love.
We will carry the love with us.
Jesus has come into the world to give us joy and praising, singing
and dancing:
That all may know that Jesus has come into the world.

SECOND SUNDAY OF CHRISTMAS

(if before 6 January)

Jeremiah 31.7–14 (alternative reading Ecclesiasticus 24.1–12);
Psalm 147.12–20 (alternative canticle Wisdom of Solomon 10.15–21);
Ephesians 1.3–14; John 1.(1–9) 10–18

THE PROMISE IS FULFILLED!

Presentation
*Illustration: a flourishing garden. Demonstrate and discuss the
difference between a bucket of sand and a well-tended pot plant.
Draw out the importance of environment, cultivation, care and
commitment in the creation of a beautiful garden. Christ is God's
nurturing and nourishing care for us, not only urging us to change,
but making that transformation possible – if we co-operate.*

(40) Call to Worship

Psalm 147.1, 12–13 *or* Jeremiah 31.7, 10.

(41) Prayer of Adoration

We praise you, Lord, we proclaim your grace,
for you have saved us, your people, and gathered us here;
caring for the weak and the frail,
and turning our griefs into joys:
We praise you, Lord God, we adore you.

We praise you, Lord, we proclaim your grace,
for you have fulfilled your promise to us, your people;
consoling those who weep, befriending the lonely,
refreshing those who thirst in spirit,
and leading the wanderers home:
We praise you, Lord God, we adore you.

We praise you, Lord, we proclaim your grace,
for your radiance has illumined our night,
and you have brought us from poverty to abundance;
a time of giving and feasting, riches and laughter,
light and gladness, joy and dancing:
We praise you, Lord God, we adore you.

(42) Prayer of Confession

O Christ the Light, you come to us as Word, as Wisdom,
as God's creative life yearning to do a new thing in the world.
But we like our own ideas and ways; we prefer to remain pure;
we remain within our circle because we want to know who is on
  our side.
Silence.

O Christ the Light, you come to us as Truth, as Glory.
You tell us our story, but in a way we have not heard before.
You show us that our tradition was larger than we had imagined.
You understand our experience, but you lead us beyond it.
And it frightens us. We do not want to recognize ourselves like
  this.
So we turn aside from knowing; we do not want you close;
we refuse to place in you our trust;
we drown out your song with a clamour of our own.
Silence.

O Christ the Light, you come to us as the power to change,
the strengthening grace to be different,
to live an alternative future, and to transform the world.
May we grow into wiser versions of ourselves,
seeking your fullness, your maturity, your freedom,
that wisdom and grace may be made flesh in us,
and we may witness to your glory.

(43) Prayer of Thanksgiving

Thanks be to God,
for bread and word to feed body and mind;
love and prayer to nourish heart and soul;
and for the cleansing of the Spirit meeting our spirit:
Thanks be to God.

Thanks be to God,
for the lavishness of provision,
for the promise fulfilled,
and for the wonder of our inheritance in Christ:
Thanks be to God.

Thanks be to God,
who has chosen us in love,
trained us in compassion,
and who sustains us in faith and hope:
Thanks be to God.

(44) Prayer of Petition

Living God, your love flows throughout creation,
boundless and free, without limit or constraint,
except where you are resisted and refused:
Immerse us in the flow of your healing waters.

You would fold all in the grace of your compassionate purpose,
lavishing upon us the riches of companionship,
the mercy of forgiveness, the joyous pain of service:
Carry us on your river of peace.

You have given us insights into the unplumbed depths of your
mystery. We bear a knowledge of your wisdom and your intent,
that desire which would bring all into your liberation and your joy:
**Draw us beyond the shore of your promise known into the sea
of adoring praise.**

(45) Prayer of Dedication

O God of the transforming Spring,
well up within our hearts
as life, as love, as peace, as joy;
that new hopes may be sown in the world.
May others' hearts find refreshment through us,
and through our weeding, digging, planting
in the soil of our daily lives,
may gardens grow in ruined towns and desert places.

(46) Prayer of Dismissal

Let us receive the blessing of God, for the promise is fulfilled and
our hope is come. Let us live in rejoicing, for the promise is
fulfilled, and God's joy is ours. Let us offer the grace of God, for
the promise is fulfilled, and all are invited to the feast of life.

EPIPHANY (6 January)

Isaiah 60.1–6; Psalm 72.(1–7) 10–14; Ephesians 3.1–12;
Matthew 2.1–12

SEARCHING FOR GOD

Presentation

*Illustration: a treasure hunt. Set a task which encourages people to
'search' and to 'find' some hidden 'treasure' in the church. Offer
some clues, as appropriate. Discuss how we go about searching.
Where do we find the clues which will lead us to the discovery? How
might we be led astray? How do we feel when we discover what we
wished to find? Link this with the story of the magi, and with our own
experiences of seeking, and discovering, God.*

(47) Call to Worship

Isaiah 60.1–3 *or* Psalm 72.18–19.

(48) Prayer of Adoration

O God of majesty, we adore you,
for you have made known to us the mystery of the ages,
you have revealed to us your love in Christ,
your Spirit is leading us into all truth.
We praise you, O God, we adore you:
We will sing our love and joy.

O God of splendour, we adore you,
for you have called us to speak of your wonders,
and you are uniting us as the body of your Son,
so that we can witness to your grace before earth and heaven.
We praise you, O God, we adore you:
We will sing our love and joy.

O God of glory, we adore you,
for you have made us heirs of your promise.
Through your Son we can enter your holy presence,
and we proclaim a realm of peace where all people belong.
We praise you, O God, we adore you:
We will sing our love and joy.

(49) Prayer of Confession

Lord God, we call you our King,
but faced with the mystery of your purposes,
riches we can never fully explore,
we know only too well our need of help
and a new start.
Silence.

Wise men travelled through cities, spoke to politicians,
followed the star-sign, gave of their treasure –
We cannot do that. We do not have enough wisdom, faith or love.
May we come then (like the wise men at least in this)
and find you as a child . . .
Silence.

Then we would come quietly: with awe, but not afraid;
with joy, maybe pain – tears in our laughter.
We have no precious gifts, but we will kneel, the better to see you,
and, forgetting ourselves a moment,
dare to reach out and touch your small, warm hand.

(50) Prayer of Thanksgiving

Thanks be to God: for festivity, fun and food;
for music, rest and good company;
for reunions, homecomings and new beginnings;
for friends and family in joy and in sadness;
for loneliness eased, work well done, reconciliations attempted;
for glimpses of love in all of these – Thanks be to God!

(51) Meditation or Prayer of Dedication

Holy Child of Bethlehem, we come seeking the joy of your birth,
but find in your humility a foreshadowing of your cross.
We arrive bearing gifts, but, shamed by your poverty,
become aware of our own empty hands.

We are looking for life, and we find it,
life for each one of us, life unlimited, life beyond our imagining,
life beyond the death that we also find,
here in this offering of blood and flesh and pain.

(52) Prayer of Dismissal

Go then: the way ahead may seem uncertain, and your path dark, but the star of your King shines on. You do not journey alone. Love is waiting at each corner. Joy lies ahead.

SUNDAY BETWEEN 7 AND 13 JANUARY

(First Sunday in Ordinary Time. This Sunday may be observed as Covenant Sunday)

Isaiah 42.1–9; Psalm 29; Acts 10.34–43; Matthew 3.13–17

COVENANT OF JOY

Presentation

Illustration: a passport. Read the pledges which are contained on the inside front cover (within some congregations, this should be handled with sensitivity, as it will raise painful issues surrounding citizenship and nationality). Discuss the idea of contract and allegiance implied here: that loyalty operates (ideally) in two directions. God pledges faithfulness to us and we offer allegiance to God. What does God ask? What does God promise in return? With what kind of power are we protected? What commission are we called upon to perform in God's name?

(53) Call to Worship

Psalm 29.1–2, Isaiah 42.1 or 1–4; *or the following acclamation*:

Praise God's holy name! Praise God's great splendour!
The voice of God is mighty! The voice of God is powerful!
The voice of God is majesty! The voice of God uproots the trees!
The voice of God moves mountains! The voice of God is flashing
    fire! The voice of God is thunder!
Our God is like a whirlwind! Our God is like a tempest!
Our God is ruler of the flood! Our God will rule for ever!
Our God will give us strength and hope!
Our God will give us life and peace! Praise God! Praise God!

This version of Psalm 29 can be chanted, with the congregation feeding back each line after the leader: or the original psalm can be read with sound effects (e.g. clapping, gongs, wobble boards, shakers etc.)

(54) Prayer of Adoration

Loving God, you have announced to us a new thing: a time of marvels and an age of praise. And we gather to wonder at the love which has been part of your creative purpose for us since before the world began:
We praise you, loving God.

Loving God, you have revealed to us a new thing: a child of hope, a child of joy. And we celebrate with awe the gentleness of your dealings with us, for you are tender and humble, vulnerable and wise:
We praise you, loving God.

Loving God, you have called us as witnesses to your new thing: to pray in trust and to sing our faith. So we declare the holiness and justice with which you guide the path of nations, drawing us all into freedom and praise:
We praise you, loving God.

(55) Meditation or Prayer of Acknowledgment

Quieten our spirits, whispering God,
that we may hear the thin thread of your voice
speaking in silences and words unsaid.
For you will not interrupt or override our ramblings
but prefer to wait within the hush
beyond the limits of our speech.

Humble our spirits, gentle God,
that we may learn your frailty among the broken and the weak;
your love which does not claim its rights;
your peace which stands aside
to let the fragile candle know itself a flame.

(56) Prayer of Thanksgiving

Give thanks to God, who is all love and goodness, mercy and
kindness. In grace we are called into life:
God is Lord of all.
Give thanks to God, who is all strength and healing, forgiveness
and comfort. In grace we are called to die with Christ:
God is Lord of all.
Give thanks to God, who is all deliverance and renewal, freedom
and fulfilment. In grace we are called to resurrection:
God is Lord of all.
Give thanks to God, who is all faithfulness, and who guides us,
feeds us and keeps us as we live out our baptism. In grace we are
called to sacrifice and transformation:
God is Lord of all.

(57) Prayer of Dedication

Faithful God, holding us in your steadfast love,
feeding us on the bread of your own life, choosing us as your
people, your priests, your witnesses before the world:
We will live to the praise of your glory.

Loving God, preparing us by your example,
guiding us with your wisdom, calling us as your disciples, your
ambassadors, messengers of your good news to all humanity:
We will live to the praise of your glory.

Glorious God, leading us toward new horizons,
enlarging our faith, our hope, our love; urging us on as your
servants, your ministers, bearers of your grace throughout the earth:
We will live to the praise of your glory.

(58) Prayer of Dismissal

Bless us, Lord of truth, that we may remain true to your trust in us
in all our daily living. Remain with us, Lord of life, that we may
keep faith with you, sharing your grace with all whose lives touch
ours.

SUNDAY BETWEEN 14 AND 20 JANUARY

(Second Sunday in Ordinary Time: This Sunday may fall within the Octave of Prayer for Christian Unity)

Isaiah 49.1–7; Psalm 40.1–11; I Corinthians 1.1–9; John 1.29–42

WHAT DO YOU SEE?

Presentation
Illustration: a jigsaw puzzle. A pile of jigsaw pieces contain all the necessary elements, but we cannot see the picture. Does it match the picture on the box? In order to see the picture as a whole we have to get involved, we have to do the puzzle. To sort out what is real, we have to get involved, get engaged, get closer. Draw out how this is also true of Christian discipleship. What might prevent us from getting involved with Jesus – fear, pride, ignorance? How are these to be overcome to free us for following Christ where he would lead us?

(59) Call to Worship

Psalm 40.1–3; Isaiah 49.5–6; I Corinthians 1.1–3; John 1.32–34; *or the following:*

Let us worship God who has saved us, drawing us out of the mire of wrong to stand firm on the rock of Christ.
Let us worship God!
Let us worship God who redeems us, calling us out of concern for ourselves to rejoice as a people of praise.
Let us worship God!

(60) Prayer of Adoration

With the grace of gratitude we adore you,
For you have magnified your blessings towards us,
revealing to us your love and mercy.
We have seen your glory: **We adore you.**

With the grace of humility we adore you.
For you have given us a readiness to learn from you,
and enriched us with wisdom and knowledge.
We have seen your glory: **We adore you.**

With the grace of love we adore you.
For you have called us to belong to Christ and to each other,
trusting in your eternal faithfulness towards us.
We have seen your glory: **We adore you.**

(61) Prayer of Confession

Forgive us, God of grace, that though you have called us into unity,
we have continued our divisions, strengthened our distrust,
reinforced attitudes of separation, and passed on our prejudices to
others.

Call us again in mercy, that we may be one in compassion, service
and praise, and so witness to your love, your grace, your glory.

(62) Prayer of Thanksgiving

O God our Deliverer,
Because you have seen our desire to pray,
you have put a new song into our mouth:
We will speak of your goodness O God.
We will witness to your love.

Because you have seen our desolation,
you have filled us with the light of your hope:
We will speak of your goodness O God.
We will witness to your love.

Because you have seen our burden of care,
you have refreshed us with your presence:
We will speak of your goodness O God.
We will witness to your love.

Because you have seen our loneliness,
you have given us the grace of companionship:
We will speak of your goodness O God.
We will witness to your love.

Because you have seen our faltering steps,
you have placed our feet upon a solid foundation:
We will speak of your goodness O God.
We will witness to your love.

(63) Prayer of Petition or Dedication

Bear our concerns upon your heart, merciful God our creator, for
you have pledged your faith to us. In Christ you have given us your
holy allegiance. Through the Spirit you have engaged your life to
our wellbeing.

And we would not fail you, though we are not always listening, and
we are easily distracted towards what is false.
Purify our hearing, our acting and our praying, that our serving
may be a ready response to your grace, love given for love.

(64) Prayer of Dismissal

May the sustaining grace of our faithful God surround us. May the
humble holiness of our brother Jesus call us to be more like him.
May the common bond of the Spirit give a strong purpose to all we
do together. And may the powerful peace of our God, Father, Son
and Spirit, fill our hearts, our homes and our world.

SUNDAY BETWEEN 21 AND 27 JANUARY

(Third Sunday in Ordinary Time. This Sunday may fall within the Octave of Prayer for Christian Unity)

Isaiah 9.1–4; Psalm 27.1, 4–9; I Corinthians 1.10–18; Matthew 4.12–23

GUIDING LIGHT

Presentation
Illustration: 'cat's eyes' in the road, lighthouses. Draw out how these lights guide us through adverse conditions, keep us in the right way, warn us of dangers. But do we know – or care – where our journey is going? Or who our companions might be? Or what hazards we might face along the way? Or how we are to be sustained and fed? How can the guiding light of God's grace and love help us in the pilgrimage we face in daily life? Or in reconciliation with others?

(65) Call to Worship

Psalm 27.1, 5; Isaiah 9.1–2.

(66) Prayer of Adoration

Stranger God – approaching us not only as a familiar friend, but as the person we do not know at all:
We praise you.
Unexpected God – challenging us not only through the word that warms our hearts, but also through the word that sears our souls:
We praise you.
Outsider God – crying out to us as the foreigner within our gates, and the enemy for whom we must pray:
We praise you.
Mysterious God – remaining beyond us in light and glory, drawing us deeper into a life beyond our imagination:
We praise you.

(67) Prayer of Confession

O God of endless love, we have lost our way in a fog of busyness and forgetfulness. We have strayed from your road. We have followed false guides. Your face of joy seems hidden from us, your wisdom is obscured from us. We are tired, divided, oppressed.

Come to us again, God of endless love. Lead us as those who belong to you. Lead us as those who are called into your community of sharing. Establish us in justice and hope. Guide our steps into your way of peace.

(68) Prayer of Thanksgiving

Pilgrim God, yours is the light that keeps us
through oppression, cruelty, imprisonment.
Yours is the light of justice:
We give you thanks and praise.

Pilgrim God, yours is the light that remains with us
even when we are encircled by hostility.
Yours is the light of freedom:
We give you thanks and praise.

Pilgrim God, yours is the light of refuge
when we are pursued by determined enemies.
Yours is the light of hope:
We give you thanks and praise.

Pilgrim God, yours is the light of truth
when we are distracted by temptation, trapped by grief or despair,
betrayed by falsehood.
Yours is the light of holiness:
We give you thanks and praise.

(69) Meditation or Prayer of Dedication

Jesus Wayfarer, lead us on
to your appointed hour of Cross and Rising,
to your determined place of pain and glory,
to your committed offering of energy and dream.
Lead us on: though we do not know the day or the moment,
though we do not know ourselves, though we do not know the way.
Lead us on: through mist and tempest, fire and storm,
lead us on together. Lead us home.

(70) Prayer of Dismissal

As we follow you step by step, loving God, hold us in your care.
As we struggle to remain true to your love in word and deed, hold
us in your peace. As we seek your way of peace in a frightened and
frightening world, hold us in your joy.

SUNDAY BETWEEN 28 JANUARY AND 3 FEBRUARY

(Fourth Sunday in Ordinary Time)

Micah 6.1–8; Psalm 15; I Corinthians 1.18–31; Matthew 5.1–12

UPSIDE DOWN GOD

Presentation
Illustration: the story of the King's new clothes. Draw out how it was the child who was able to see – and speak for – reality and truth. God sees situations as they really are, but in order to see the world as God sees it, we usually have to turn our ideas, priorities and concerns upside down. How can our faith in Christ help us to see reality? And can those outcast from society help us to see – and speak for – what is really important?

(71) Call to Worship

Micah 6.6a, 8; *or the following:*

Come into the presence of God,
as those who are seeking to serve with faithfulness,
as those who are pure in heart and mind,
as those who are true to God's purposes.

Come into the presence of God,
as you are, and as you would be,
and know that you are loved for yourselves,
and for your great desire, today and forever.

(72) Prayer of Adoration

Praise Christ – who has turned upside down the wisdom of the
    world.
Praise Christ – who has saved us by a degrading death.
Praise Christ – who has hung before us in terrible vulnerability.
Praise Christ – who turns in shame from the complacent comfort of
    his church, but shares in the laughter of the dying, links arms
    with those who dance on the fringes of respectability, and weeps
    in the shadows, where, with those who do not even merit a
    name, he makes his home.

(73) Prayer of Confession and Thanksgiving

Wise and loving God, we have failed to see ourselves as we are; we have failed to understand the depth of your love for us and for all people; we have failed to discern your priorities for the right ordering of your realm of hope. In your grace, forgive us.
Silence.

Wise and loving God, we ask that we may see you clearly; uncluttered by the debris of past failings; unfettered by the clinging strands of false loyalties, by the knots of prejudice, by the deceits of power. In your grace, purify our sight.
Silence.

Wise and loving God, we thank you for the wisdom of your small ones, your least disciples, your poor. Grant us courage to learn poverty, that we may discover your riches; to become foolish, so that we may speak with your wisdom; to celebrate weakness, resting in your strength; to rejoice in being nothing, because Christ has become all things.

(74) Prayer of Dedication

Loving Wisdom of God, keep us in the hurting place where we can offer our grief as your tears for the suffering of people overwhelmed by war, famine or oppression.

Hold us in the hurting place, when we would prefer to run away or hide our guilt and pain in sweet songs or easy giving.

Challenge us in the hurting place through the faith of elderly men and women, the wholeness of the diseased, and the insights of a child.

Teach us in the hurting place what it means to pray when no sign appears to mark your presence or your approval, and no wonder serves to strengthen our faith against indifference.

Loving Wisdom of God, keep us, hold us, challenge us, teach us in the hurting places of our age, that through our patience and our faithfulness, your grace may be offered for the healing of the world.

Prayers of Dismissal

(75)
Go out into God's world,
as those who are seeking to serve with faithfulness,
as those who are pure in heart and mind,
as those who are true to God's purposes.
Go out into God's world,
as you are, and as you would be,
and know that you are loved for yourselves,
and for your great desire, today and forever.

(76)
May the God of grace lead us into deeper offering.
May the God of holiness grant us greater integrity.
May the God whose folly is wiser than the wisdom of the world,
and whose weakness is stronger than any human strength,
keep us in truth:
that we may find the home prepared for us,
this day and forever.

SUNDAY BETWEEN 4 AND 10 FEBRUARY

(Fifth Sunday in Ordinary Time)

Isaiah 58.1–9a (9b–12); Psalm 112.1–9 (10);
I Corinthians 2.1–12 (13–16); Matthew 5.13–20

SALT OF THE EARTH

Presentation

Illustration: salt, and salty items such as crisps or fish preserved in brine. Discuss how salt is used in the flavouring and preserving of food, and in the cleaning and healing of wounds. Its saltiness is its essential nature – without this it is useless. Draw out, too, how salt is not only a necessary ingredient, but also a noticeable one, even though it is often hidden. Being noticed is also part of its essential nature. What might this analogy teach us about the nature and value of our Christian faith within our families, our neighbourhood, our world?

(77) Call to Worship

Psalm 112.1–2 *or* Isaiah 58.8–9a; *or the following:*

Come to us, compassionate Creator, and speak to our inmost souls,
that we may hear your word addressing our secret hopes and fears.
Come to us, Jesus our Brother, and show how you lived amongst us,
that we may see your faith, your hope, your love,
made real in our own thoughts and words and deeds.
Come to us, wise Spirit, and mould us as one Body,
that we may have the mind of Christ,
and give glory to you, one God, this day and forever.

(78) Prayer of Adoration

O loving heart of God, made weak that we might be strengthened
by your vulnerable compassion: **We praise you.**
O loving mind of Christ, made fearful that we might be encouraged
by your humble obedience: **We praise you.**
O loving Spirit, coming to us in trembling tenderness that we might
be comforted by your gentle power: **We praise you.**

(79) Prayer of Confession

Merciful God, forgive the depth of our rebellion against you,
for we have not lived in holiness or purity of heart.
We have said prayers, sung hymns, and spoken of you
but we have failed to do right things, to practise righteousness.
We have expected you to be holy, just and good,
but we have not expected these standards of ourselves.
We have disobeyed your teaching, our humility has been
self-serving, our generosity has been for our own glory; we have
made a god of our religion, and have accepted the presence of
conflict and violence.
O God of mercy, forgive us.
Silence.

Merciful God, teach us how to follow you in radical holiness,
how to live from glad and generous hearts.
Show us how to be a flavoursome and purifying presence
wherever we live and work for you.
Help us to enrich and enhance the lives of those around us.
May your love, through us, challenge and transform
all relationships and systems in our community,
and may we serve you as a people of honesty and praise.

(80) Prayer of Thanksgiving

For your secret wisdom, made available to all in Christ Jesus,
we give you thanks and praise.
For your hidden power, poured out on all peoples
as sacrificial generosity and resurrection grace,
we give you thanks and praise.
For your mystery, revealed for all time in an offering of faithful
obedience, we give you thanks and praise.

(81) Prayer of Dedication

Liberating God, you have called us to the urgent task
of seeing where you are at work in the world,
amongst those who are shut out, and those who have nothing.
And you have called us to the complex task
of discerning how the tangled webs of hatred, oppression and
deceit are to be unpicked and cut,
so that the hungry are fed, the naked clothed,
the homeless housed, and the stranger welcomed.
**Receive us again as your servants and co-workers in a mission
which will require of us everything in passion and persistence.
Let your Spirit be a well of strength and understanding in our
midst, that we may be faithful to your purposes and give glory
to your Name, this day and forever.**

(82) Prayer of Dismissal

Go into your daily life as salt, to preserve what is good, to bring
out the best in others, and to cleanse all things with love.
Go into your daily life as salt, to be God's people hidden amongst
the nations, yet available and offered to all the world.

SUNDAY BETWEEN 11 AND 17 FEBRUARY

(Sixth Sunday in Ordinary Time)

Deuteronomy 30.15–20 (Ecclesiasticus 15.15–20);
Psalm 119.1–8; I Corinthians 3.1–9; Matthew 5.21–37

WHICH WAY?

Presentation
Illustration: signpost pointing in three directions (choose three local placenames). Discuss how we decide which road to choose, drawing out that it depends on our proposed destination. Then change the names on the signpost to read: (a) Backwards (b) Our way (c) God's way. If (a) represents where we have come from, how do we decide which of the other roads to take? Discuss what factors might affect our choice. Again, the final decision depends on where we are going.

(83) Call to Worship

Psalm 119.1–3 *or* Deuteronomy 30.15–16.

(84) Prayer of Adoration

God of all creation, you are our goal and our glory,
our heaven and our hearts' desire:
May we walk in your way of love.
You have set before us, as inspiration and example,
the life and death and resurrection of your Son, Jesus Christ,
and called us to follow in his footsteps:
May we walk in your way of love.
You draw us on, teaching us how to live in justice, truth and peace,
and strengthening us through the Holy Spirit.
You will never abandon us:
May we walk in your way of love.

(85) Prayer of Confession

Before using this prayer, encourage the congregation to reflect in silence on some of the wrong choices they have made. If there is a high level of mutual trust within the group, such reflections could be shared.

O Living God, you have set before us this day, as every day, the choices which come from being alive and active in the world.
Life – or death.
Faithfulness – or fickleness.
Holiness – or wickedness.
Obedience – or obstinacy.
Purity – or corruption.
Blessing – or curse.

Today, as every day, we must choose between alternatives.
Sometimes we choose well, sometimes we make mistakes.
Sometimes we make bad choices in good faith.
Sometimes we turn aside from what we know is right.
Today, as every day, we lean on your mercy, and trust in your
    grace.
We know that we have done wrong things in the past.
We know that we will not always get it right in the future.
But we ask that you will prompt us, guide us, teach us and lead us,
and help us to prompt, guide, teach and lead each other,
so that with our eyes fixed on your love and grace,
we may know that you have forgiven us,
even as we are learning to forgive one another.

(86) Prayer of Thanksgiving or Dismissal

God is with us in the places of decision:
Praise to the living God!
God is with us in the moments of hard choosing:
Praise to the living God!
God is with us in our times of temptation:
Praise to the living God!
God is with us to the end of the journey:
Praise to the living God!

(87) Meditation or Prayer of Petition

Help us to live, O God of growing,
not from the outward, edgy parts of ourselves,
the bits that stick out, snagging on the fabric of life,
and tearing at other peoples' feelings.
For we can be sharp, awkward, difficult shapes
to fit into the pattern of your creation.
We bump people and bruise them where they are already tender.
We make ourselves into obstacles, and they fall over us.
Rather, help us to live from that inward spring
of your love which you have placed inside us,
and which keeps on flowing,
smoothing its channel as it passes through,
moulding, melting and dissolving,
rubbing away our spikes and rounding off our corners,
so that we may offer ourselves to your creative service
not as stumbling blocks but as healing waters.

(88) Prayer of Dedication

Hold our hearts in your grace, compassionate God,
that we may no longer be content with half a faith,
with luke-warm commitment, or with an offering
of the minimum and the least.
Hold our hearts in your grace:
For we need your supporting care.

Hold our lives in your hand, protecting God,
that we may not faint or falter when our road becomes hard,
or the choices difficult to make.
Grant us the wisdom to choose your alternative,
even if it seems the harder, costlier way.
Hold our lives in your hand:
For we need your supporting care.

Hold our dreams in your dream, joyous God,
that we may not lose hope or courage,
but be constantly renewed in passion and generosity.
May we accompany others in their walk of life,
and together come to the fulfilment of your promises.
Hold our dreams in your dream:
For we need your supporting care.

SUNDAY BETWEEN 18 AND 24 FEBRUARY

(Seventh Sunday in Ordinary Time)

Leviticus 19.1–2, 9–18; Psalm 119.33–40;
I Corinthians 3.10–11, 16–23; Matthew 5.38–48

COPYING GOD

Presentation
*Illustration: 'original' items and copies of them. Talk about the
different types of 'original' which might be copied (documents,
books, statues, paintings) and how changes in technology have
enabled us to make more and better copies (printing, photocopying,
computers). What aspects of God are we urged to copy? What is it
that enables us to become 'copies of God'?*

(89) Call to Worship

Psalm 119.33–35 *or* Leviticus 19.1–2, *or the following:*

Show us your way, teacher God, and lead us in the path of your
    instruction:
We will be faithful to the end of our days.
Show us your heart, loving God, and give us the desire to follow
    you:
We will be faithful to the end of our days.
Show us yourself, holy God, and fill us with your life:
We will be faithful to the end of our days.

(90) Prayer of Adoration

O God of all glory: yours is a broad and understanding love,
a persevering compassion, a merciful and impartial grace.
You always see the human being behind the problem,
the person behind the evil deed.
You do not stand on ceremony, or on your own dignity,
or quarrel about each infringement of your rights,
but spend yourself in generosity to all,
regardless of whether or not we are grateful.

Yours is a giving which includes everyone – brothers, sisters,
neighbours, enemies, friends – none are beyond your reach,
all are gathered into your embrace.
Your one longing is to pour out blessing on all creation,
until the day when the universe is drawn into a single joy.

(91) Prayer of Confession

For all the wrong in our attitude to others and to you:
Merciful Father, forgive us.
For the shabbiness of our worship and our neglect of those in need:
Merciful Father, forgive us.
For the way we deceive ourselves and try to deceive others:
Merciful Father, forgive us.
For our petty disputes over rights and responsibilities:
Merciful Father, forgive us.
For our unthinking cruelty towards the problems and pain of others:
Merciful Father, forgive us.
For the ease with which we think ill of our neighbour:
Merciful Father, forgive us.
For our willingness to bear grudges and seek vengeance:
Merciful Father, forgive us.
For our co-operation with systems of oppression and those who
continue injustice:
Merciful Father, forgive us.

(92) Prayer of Petition

Make us copies of yourself, holy God.
Question our motives, challenge our excuses.
Touch our hearts, and turn us around
so that all we are is measured by your love
and caught up in the movement of your grace.
Help us understand your teachings:
We will keep them to the end.

Re-create us in your image, holy God.
Awaken our talents, purify our ambitions.
Consecrate our minds, and receive the offering
of our dedicated lives, that we may be complete
in all our praying, loving, giving, for your sake.
Help us understand your teachings:
We will keep them to the end.

*Build us as your temples, holy God.
Claim our devotion, govern our allegiance.
Take up all our longings into your great desire,
that we may reflect your generosity to all creation.
Help us understand your teachings:
We will keep them to the end.

* *This paragraph may be used, or repeated, as a prayer of
dedication.*

(93) Prayer of Dedication or Dismissal

Call us again, O God, to that essential holiness
which is a heart of compassion, a mind of purity,
a zeal for justice and a spirit of praise:
**We will praise you with joyous hearts
as we learn how to obey your word.**

SUNDAY BETWEEN 25 AND 29 FEBRUARY

(Eighth Sunday in Ordinary Time)

Isaiah 49.8–16a; Psalm 131; I Corinthians 4.1–5; Matthew 6.24–34

GOD WHO PROVIDES

Presentation
Illustration: a tray or table set for morning tea/coffee. Talk through the process which has led up to the provision of this simple refreshment: laying the tray, making the tea/coffee, buying the ingredients, earning the money to pay for them, manufacturing the products, growing the food etc. At which points in the process can we be conscious of God's providing love? Can valuing God's part in the process also help us to value those others who have had a part in it? What are the implications of this for our family relationships? Our work? The rights of others?

(94) Call to Worship

Psalm 131 (read with a silence between verses 2 and 3) *or* Isaiah 49.13, 16a.

(95) Prayer of Adoration and Thanksgiving

Father-Mother God,
with all your creation we thank you for your nourishment and care;
for the gentleness of your guidance,
for the urgency of your call,
for the strength which lowers the road and smooths the way,
for the springs of your renewing Spirit.
Sing for joy all the earth:
For our God will provide for us!

Father-Mother God,
with all your people we thank you
for the intimacy of your concern for us;
for your knowledge of our needs,
for your delight in our company,

for the costly offering of your life for our health and growing,
for the warmth of your compassion.
Sing for joy all the earth:
For our God will provide for us!

Father-Mother God,
with all your church we thank you
for your steadfast love for us:
for you accept us as we really are,
you understand us when we are weak,
and forgive us when we say sorry;
you are interested in the details of our daily lives,
and you encourage us with kindness.
Sing for joy all the earth:
For our God will provide for us!

(96) Meditation or Prayer of Acknowledgment

Silence. Or Psalm 131 may be read by another voice.

Mothering God, yours is a peace which quietens us,
calming our anxieties, quelling our fears,
laying the hand of love upon all our panic and impatience,
relaxing us with your presence and your peace.
You ask us to be humble, lowly and dependent,
content, like a child, to be held in your embrace,
grateful, like a child, to be welcomed.
You are concerned for the small, the humdrum and the mundane
moments of our everyday. You love us in details,
you enjoy us at the kitchen sink, and at the garage workshop,
in the absorption of hobbies and the satisfaction of work well done.
You offer yourself for our nourishment,
inviting us to draw on you for our hope, our renewal and our praise.
For when we wander far away, you call us back,
and when we feel cut off from love, you gather us together.
You protect us from the scorching wind of the desert,
and refresh us with the living springs of your Spirit.
Our faces and our needs are always before you.
Our sorrows and our joys your constant concern.
You hold us in your memory:
like the child of the heart,
and the name written on the hand.

(97) Prayer of Petition

Bring forward that day, Judge of all the world, when we shall give account to you, as your servants, and with all humanity come before you for the scrutiny of our deeds:
Have mercy on us and hear our prayer.

Bring forward that day when all the evil which is done in secret, all the crimes which are concealed from justice, and all the lies that are told, will be exposed, and your truth no longer hidden or disguised:
Have mercy on us and hear our prayer.

Bring forward that day when hypocrisy will be laid bare, and the purposes of the heart revealed; when the greatest pleasure will be taken in acts of simple goodness, and words of wisdom treasured:
Have mercy on us and hear our prayer.

Bring forward that day for the liberation of the oppressed, and the restoration of those whose dignity has been destroyed. May that day be your answer to injustice and to the cries of the poor:
Have mercy on us and hear our prayer.

Bring forward that day, and have mercy, Judge of all the world, that it may be a day of healing and light, when wrongs are put right, and pain is relieved, when bitterness is purged away, and suffering is understood. Bring forward that day, that the cleansing of your forgiveness may flow through us:
Have mercy on us and hear our prayer.

(98) Prayer of Dedication

Help us, God of love, to come to you
trusting in your wisdom to know us and your care to provide for us.
Receive now our offering;
that we may pledge to you our gifts, our devotion and our lives,
that your realm may be built in our community,
and your rule be established in our hearts.

(99) Prayer of Dismissal

Go into the plenty of God's creation, grateful for all that is provided for you, just in your use of all that is given, and generous in forgiveness, faith and adoration.

SUNDAY BEFORE LENT

Exodus 24.12–18; Psalm 2 (or Psalm 99); II Peter 1.16–21;
Matthew 17.1–9

WE WERE THERE!

Presentation
*Illustration: a ticket or programme for a football match or concert,
or an eye-witness newspaper report of a memorable event. Talk
about the excitement and sense of involvement which comes from
having witnessed an important happening. Draw out how such
involvement can draw people together, and the responsibility on the
witness to testify to the truth of the event. How might we be changed
by being a witness – or through the witness of others?*

(100) Call to Worship

Psalm 2.7–8 *or* Psalm 99.1–3, 9 *or* 1–5.

(101) Prayer of Adoration

O God of uncreated power,
from the depths of glory you call to us, drawing us into the bright
cloud of your love, inviting us into a mystery of communion:
God of glory, we adore you.

O God of majesty,
in your awesome purity you summon us to stand with all your saints
in your holy presence, though all that is sin in us cannot endure the
touch of your devouring fire:
God of truth, we adore you.

O God of eternity,
with unlimited patience you incline our hearts to await the hour of
your purpose, when all the tangled threads of time are woven into
the perfect moment of your grace:
O God of all seasons, we adore you.

O God of plenty,
from the generosity of your overflowing heart you pour out the
blessings of healing light upon all people, upon all the world:
O God of abundance, we adore you.

(102) Prayer of Acknowledgment

God of peace,
in the waiting, which seems endless,
for your promise of justice to be fulfilled
for the poor, the persecuted and the oppressed:
School us in patience, fortitude and zeal.

As we wait with you in obscurity, for your truth to be revealed:
Prompt us to hear you and obey your teachings.

In the interval while violence and cruelty hold sway
over those who cannot defend themselves,
and when those who would help them are overwhelmed:
Strengthen us to stand fast for what is right.

In these days when your teaching is flouted,
your instruction ignored, your commandments broken,
and your law cast into the mire of our indifference:
Grant us to revere your purposes and celebrate your acts.

And in the fullness of time, when all your work is complete,
your plans brought to fruition, and the fragments of your dream
brought into one:
**Gather us with the broken pieces of your making,
into the glorious crown of your new creation.**

(103) Prayer of Thanksgiving

Thank you, loving God, that as you call us higher up the mountain,
so you are revealing to us more of your truth, your hope, your
endless joy.
Thank you, gracious God, that as you call us deeper into the
mystery of your compassion, so you are renewing us with your
strength, your humility, your eternal peace.

(104) Prayer of Dedication

Creator God, with the first disciples we stand on the mountaintop
dazed by light and the sudden enlargement of our vision.
We have seen what we did not expect to see –
that Jesus is greater than we have realized,
greater than we could have known:
We have seen the glory: we are witnesses.

Father God, with the first disciples we listen in awe to a
conversation of ancient wisdom, of telling and prophetic word.
The promises are made sure, and our faith is made strong in hope.
Your teaching is greater than we have realized,
greater than we could have known:
We have seen the glory: we are witnesses.

Saviour God, with the first disciples we long to remain here, secure
in this special place, set apart in this holy place.
We have become what we did not expect to become.
Your faith in us is greater than we have realized,
greater than we could have known:
We have seen the glory: we are witnesses.

(105) Prayer of Dismissal

God calls us to witness to the honour of Christ:
We will acknowledge him.
God calls us to witness to the glory of Christ:
We will commend him.
God calls us to witness to the ruling love of Christ:
We will serve him.
God calls us to witness to the suffering of Christ:
We will be his gift to all the world.

ASH WEDNESDAY

Joel 2.1–2, 12–17 (or Isaiah 58.1–12); Psalm 51.1–17;
II Corinthians 5.20b–6.10; Matthew 6.1–6

BURNING LOVE

Presentation

Illustration: fire, represented, by striking a long match. Talk about the way in which fire is used to purify as well as mould iron and precious metals. (Other examples of purification by fire might be burning garden rubbish on a bonfire or the sterilizing of medical instruments in the days before modern techniques.) As precious metals are refined in the fire, so we are refined by the work of the Holy Spirit in our lives. What is it in us which needs to be 'burned out' in the process?

(106) Call to Worship

Psalm 51.15–17 *or* Isaiah 58.8–9, *or the following:*

O Lord, open our hearts:
That we may praise you with all that we are.
O Lord, inspire our thoughts:
That we may praise you with all that we can be.
O Lord, fill our lives:
That we may praise you with all that we can offer.
O Lord, transform our community:
That we may praise you with all the world.

(107) Prayer of Adoration

God of grace, you have loved us, your people, through all the joys and sorrows of our lives, staying with us in hardship and calamity, and through the gift of Christ, showing us the depth of your love:
We adore you.

God of grace, you have cared for us, your people, through times of ease and times of difficulty, strengthening us to face harassment, mockery and persecution, and through the generosity of Christ, showing us how to pray for our enemies:
We adore you.

God of grace, you have fed us, your people, with your own
sustaining life, that we might not die but live to abundance and
eternity, and through the dying and raising of Christ, you show us
the unlimited reach of your power:
We adore you.

(108) Prayer of Confession

Compassionate God, we thank you that you are all grace and mercy
towards us; that menace and threat are not part of your nature; that
you are slow to anger and overflowing with steadfast love.

And yet we are overwhelmed by wrong, by all that is lacking in
ourselves, and by the evil in the world.

Sometimes guilt comes to us as an urgent horror, as sudden and
alarming as a trumpet-call. Sometimes it is a dull, sullen ache,
murky and obscure, a general sense of doom.

Sometimes, we know, we do not feel guilty enough, and yet at
other times it is as though we are drowning, dragged down by all
the anguish of humanity, for which we feel responsible, not only to
each other, but finally, ultimately, to you.

Holy God, we know that you do not wish pain on anyone,
however blameworthy. You yearn only to bless, and in your mercy
it is never too late in this life for us to turn again toward you,
repenting of our rebellion, and asking for forgiveness.

So for ourselves, and for the human family of which we are part,
we cry to you:
**Let the fire of your love cleanse our minds, and purify our
hearts, O God.**
**May we be honest about our shortcomings, and eager to see
your truth acknowledged in the world.**
**Forgive the wrong we have done, and the evil with which we
have co-operated.**
**Turn our wills towards your will, and transform all that is
wrong in our habits and our lives, that from this day we may
shine as witnesses to your presence, here and in all the earth.**

(109) Prayer of Petition

Let us be reconciled to God, working together with Christ in his ministry of reconciliation here and throughout the world:
Lord of mercy, receive us.
Let us not accept the grace of God in vain, for Christ is calling us to take up the Cross he offers us:
Lord of mercy, strengthen us.
Let us remember that we were bought at a cost, that Christ was humbled and shamed so that we could shine with the glory of God:
Lord of mercy, encourage us.
Let us keep hope, for as we suffer for Christ's sake, so others will come alive in him:
Lord of mercy, embolden us.
Let us go on until salvation is complete; for a day is expected when all will be judged and made right:
Lord of mercy, smooth the way, allow no obstacles to stand.

(110) Prayer of Dedication

O God of the secret way, you ask us to be people of integrity, with the zeal and ardour of our faith concealed lest we daunt and diminish those around us:
Loving God, we offer you the hidden faith,
that is seen by you alone.

O God of the secret treasure, you ask us to trust that our true life is hidden in Christ, that our dreams are honoured even when we do not see them bear fruit:
Loving God, we offer you the hidden desires,
that are seen by you alone.

O God of the secret hope, you ask us to remain true to ourselves as we are, knowing that you hear our unspoken prayers and will sustain us in readiness and joy:
Loving God, we offer you devotion of our hearts,
that is seen by you alone.

(111) Prayer of Dismissal

Hold us in your peace, loving God, through trial and testing, peril and pain, that we may receive each moment in your grace as the time of your favour, the hour of your glory.

54

FIRST SUNDAY IN LENT

Genesis 2.15–17, 3.1–7; Psalm 32; Romans 5.12–19; Matthew 4.1–11

BROKEN LIMITS

Presentation

Illustration: signs giving speed limits or other warnings from the Highway Code. Do we find it easy to drive within the limits that the code imposes on us? Why are those limits imposed? What happens if more and more people break them? Can we see the teachings of the law and of Jesus as the safety limits given by God for our good? Why might we want to break them? What might then be the consequences, for ourselves and for others?

(112) Call to worship

Genesis 2.15–17; *or* Psalm 32.7–8, 11 *could be read, as follows: Voice 1 – verse 7; voice 2 – verse 8; both voices – verse 11.*

(113)

Be glad in the Lord and rejoice,
for he has given us this earth as our home,
creating all things in goodness,
making it a place of beauty and challenge:
Be glad in the Lord and rejoice!

Be glad in the Lord and rejoice,
for he has peopled his world,
given us each other, to live in community,
to help and support, in mutual understanding:
Be glad in the Lord and rejoice!

Be glad in the Lord and rejoice,
for he has given us a Saviour;
his Son, who has freed us
from ourselves and from our wrong-doings:
Be glad in the Lord and rejoice!

Be glad in the Lord and rejoice,
for he opens the way to his heart,
paving a highway to heaven
through a vision of peace on the earth:
Be glad in the Lord and rejoice!

Be glad in the Lord and rejoice,
shout for joy!
For his kingdom is here with us – now!
Be glad in the Lord and rejoice!

(114) Prayer of Adoration

Creator God, you have breathed into us your life, and given us the
power of life and death in our relationships, in our healing, and in
administering justice:
We adore you and honour you, Creator God.

Saviour Christ, you have revealed the mystery of God's purposes
for us, and the trust we must offer in our dealings with one another:
We adore you and honour you, Saviour Christ.

Holy Spirit, you have enlightened us with wisdom and empowered
us through humble compassion, so that we might be your servants
in all creation:
We adore you and honour you, Holy Spirit.

(115) Prayer of Confession

O God of mercy, we have rebelled against your purposes,
disobeyed your instructions, and ignored your teachings.
We have broken away from your path of peace
and walked our own road, shutting our ears to your promises
and closing our hearts to your appeal.
God of joy, teach us how we should live:
God of life, look upon us with love.

O God of mercy, reach into the wasteland we have made,
for we groan under our burdens.
Speak your word of compassion into our souls,
for we have silenced hope for ourselves and the world.
Touch us again with forgiveness,
for we are hiding from your truth.
Refresh and renew our spirits,
so that our weariness is lifted, and our dry hearts may sing again.
God of joy, teach us how we should live:
God of life, look upon us with love.

(116) Prayer of Thanksgiving

Loving God, for the life that you have given,
as bread and knowledge, love and protection, presence and glory,
we give you thanks and praise.
Generous Jesus, for the life that you have given
as hunger and obedience, nakedness and vulnerability,
powerlessness and patience,
we give you thanks and praise.
Humble Spirit, for the life that you have given
wherever we live by grace and minister through sacrifice,
we give you thanks and praise.

(117) Prayer of Dedication

Father God, you set the boundaries of faith:
you call us to live within the scope of your will,
to exercise integrity,
to match our will with yours, not in bonds, but free,
free to be ourselves as you made us.

And you sent Jesus as our example.
Lord Jesus Christ, you were driven by the Spirit into the wilderness
because you needed time with God.
We need time with him, too.
Silence.

There you entered into communion with him
– he your Father, you his Son – an intimate relationship.
We need to be close to him, too.
Silence.

Yet evil was abroad. The tempter came to distract you with pangs of hunger, distorted knowledge, the possibility of power.
We suffer such distractions, too – they are part of our humanity.
Silence.

But you, Lord, had power – spiritual power – and even in your weakness you were able to use it and numb the enemy, claiming victory in God's name.
We, too, may have the victory in that name.
Silence.

Father God, you set the boundaries of faith:
you call us to live within the scope of your will,
to exercise integrity,
to match our will with yours, not in bonds, but free,
free to be ourselves as you made us.
And you sent Jesus as our example:
Strengthen us by your Holy Spirit,
that we may willingly to follow your Son,
and with him find our place in your design for the world.

(118) Prayer of Dismissal

In a time of uncertainty, live in the security that you are known and loved by our Father God.
In a time of anxiety, live in the faith you have received through the grace of Christ.
In a time of testing, live in the freedom of the Spirit, and in obedience to the generosity of God.

SECOND SUNDAY IN LENT

Genesis 12.1–4a; Psalm 121; Romans 4.1–5, 13–17; John 3.1–17

THE JOURNEY OF FAITH

Presentation

Illustration: a set of luggage containing items we might take on a journey of exploration into unknown country. Discuss: why make the journey? What do we take? What must we leave behind? Who might travel with us? What hazards might we meet? Who is our guide? Expand on this as an image of the life of faith and ask: what potential for renewal does our journey hold – for ourselves, for our community – or both?

(119) Call to Worship

Psalm 121.5–8: *the phrase* **Let us praise the Lord** *could be used as a refrain after each verse, said first by the leader, repeated by the congregation.*

(120) Prayer of Adoration

First read Psalm 121.

Lord God, you show us your glory
in ancient and familiar hills, and in skies which are new every
   sunrise.
You call us out of nowhere and make us your special people,
surrounding us with your steadfast and eternal love.
You keep us and care for us in all life's difficulties.
You guide us through tradition, but save us from being swamped
   by legality, and trust us with freedom in the sea of faith.
You show us the way of birth and rebirth,
revealing yourself to us in small things as well as great.
Lord, raise our eyes from mundane things,
and renew us, we pray:
that we may we see your glory always fresh before us
and join your saints in everlasting praise.

(121) Prayer of Confession

Nicodemus came to Jesus at night.
Forgive us when we, too, are afraid.
Silence.

Confronted by the goodness of Jesus, he found that good works
meant nothing. Forgive us when we put doing before being.
Silence.

When challenged to give up all and begin again, he could not let go.
Forgive us when possessions and achievements matter too much.
Silence.

Shown the need for a spiritual rebirth, he did not understand.
Forgive us when we resist the claims of your Spirit.
Silence.

*The prayer may be concluded with these words, or with the Prayer
of Dedication (123)*

Loving God, as we live within your forgiveness
and your renewing grace,
grant us faith as firm as that of Abraham,
conviction as strong as that of Paul,
an unwavering commitment to your service,
and a glimpse of your glory, now and hereafter.

(122) Prayer of Thanksgiving

We praise you, God of life: you are the source of all blessing for
us. From you we receive all our hope: the promise which
encourages us, the identity which sustains us, the obedience which
disciplines us, the glory which beckons us.
We praise you, God of life: you are the source of all blessing.

(123) Prayer of Dedication

You call us, Lord,
out of the comfortable niches of our lives,
out of all that is warm and familiar,
and you say, 'Come, and I will lead you into blessing.'
Lord, bless us, we pray:
That we may be a blessing to others.

You guide us, Lord,
through the mountains of our fearfulness,
through the valleys of despondency,
and you say, 'I am here, and I will bless you where you are.'
Lord, bless us, we pray:
That we may be a blessing to others.

You send us, Lord,
out into a world peopled with uncertainty,
out into a harsh and hostile environment,
and you say, 'Go, for you will always have my blessing.'
Lord, bless us, we pray:
That we may be a blessing to others.

(124) Prayer of Dismissal

God is faithful:
God who summoned Abraham,
and enabled him to answer the call:
who promised to go with him,
who led him by grace;
to this God be praise and honour
from those he calls to faith,
now and for evermore.

THIRD SUNDAY IN LENT

Exodus 17.1–7; Psalm 95; Romans 5.1–11; John 4.5–42

TESTING TIMES

Presentation

Illustration: banners of protest, with slogans such as 'No food,' 'No water,' 'No work,' etc. Who gets the blame when things go wrong in our community? How do we go about putting it right? How easy is it to retain our sense of justice and fair play? Who tends to get picked on if a scapegoat is needed? Consider how Moses, the Samaritans (in general) and the Samaritan woman (in particular) were blamed for the failures of others. At what point do we take our sense of outrage to God? How does God respond?

(125) Call to Worship

Psalm 95.1–2 or 1–3, or the following:

We come to the Lord rejoicing.
We bring our praise and thanks
for life poured out in bread and wine,
and work to do in testing times:
We come to the Lord rejoicing.
We bring our praise and thanks!

(126) Prayer of Adoration

Eternal God, we approach you with joy
as the One who saves and satisfies,
who is patient and forbearing,
who listens to your children.
Our words are inadequate to express such majestic love,
it is beyond human comprehension.
We understand earthly pomp and ceremony,
but we struggle with the concept of love
until we meet you face to face on your terms,
for you are all love.

(127) Prayer of Confession

Eternal God, we are reminded of those times when,
like Israel at Meribah, we have put you to the test.
We have argued with you and quarrelled with each other.
We have behaved like spoilt children,
spurning your gifts, refusing to share,
having no patience to wait our turn in the queue of life.
We ask you to forgive us, to stand with us in the queue,
to walk with us in the lonely ways
and help us put those faults behind us.

(128) Prayer of Thanksgiving

God of all ages, we thank you
– for your grace which is like the rod of Moses – the source of
deliverance and of blessing.
– for your generosity which sees our thirst for faith and friendship,
meaning and hope.
– for your love which is the foundation of our stability and true
security.
– for your peace which, when we allow you to be yourself in us,
makes us ready to listen and to obey.
– for the faith through which we receive your grace and share in
your glory.

(129) Prayer of Petition

The harvest fields are ripe,
peopled with empty, sick and sin-trapped souls:
Silence.
Lord, send help, we pray.

The reaper is standing by, scythe and sickle raised and ready
for that great sweep of action that will sever life
and signify a death:
Silence.
Lord, send life, we pray.

The harvester is waiting to gather in the grain.
It is cut and winnowed, the chaff separated from wholesome food:
Silence.
Lord, send love, we pray.

The sower prepares for tomorrow, ready with new seed to scatter
on fresh ground, looking towards harvest once again:
Silence.
Lord, send hope, we pray.

(130) Meditation

Christ asks only that we follow him:
through times of hardship, and to unknown destinations,
through suffering as well as to spiritual life,
to sow seed in waiting fields, already prepared,
and to be content to leave the results in others' hands.
He does not ask that we should reason why,
or make a trial of his strength,
or tease him as if he were a child.
He asks only for love.

(131) Prayer of Dedication or Dismissal

Lord of faith,
we acknowledge our great debt to you.
Grant that our faith may grow daily
as we come closer to you.
Lord of faith,
in whom we are saved to the utmost,
we commit our lives to you and your service,
in faith, this day and forever.

FOURTH SUNDAY IN LENT

(Mothering Sunday)

I Samuel 16.1–13 (Exodus 2.1–10; I Samuel 1.10–28); Psalm 23
(Psalms 34.11–20; 127.1–4); Ephesians 5.8–14 (II Corinthians 1.3–7;
Colossians 3.12–17); John 9.1–41 (Luke 2.33–35; John 19.25–27)

SEEING THE HEART

Presentation
*Illustration: a person modelling different outfits of clothes. Discuss
how we use our outward appearance to make statements about who
we are, what we like, and what is important to us. Draw out how
these statements can be the source of friction in our relationships
because of different backgrounds, generations, expectations etc.
With all this in mind, how do we go about 'seeing the heart' of a
person? What qualities and disciplines do we have to cultivate in
ourselves and our relationships if we are to see people as they really
are – and love them as they need to be loved?*

(132) Call to Worship

I Samuel 16.7; *or* Psalm 34.1–3 *or* 11–14; *or* Psalm 127.1–2, *read
by a single voice, followed by the congregational affirmation,*
We rest in the Lord, we trust in God's power.

(133)

Let us arise to meet the Light:
The Light is Christ.
Let us rejoice in the hope of this new day:
Our hope is fixed on Christ.
Let us waken to reality:
Christ is the real light.
Let us travel on into the Light:
The light for our path is Christ.

(134) Prayer of Adoration

Psalm 23 can be read in three sections (verses 1–2, verse 4, verses 5–6) separated by silence. The following phrase and response could complete each silence:
Faithful God, watching over us with tender care, we adore you:
Loving God, nourishing us with your grace, we praise your name.

(135) Prayer of Confession

Lord, we come to you confessing the failure of our relationships.
So often we have judged by outward appearances
but have not looked further into the heart
and seen the hurt of those who cannot trust,
the pain of being let down or led astray,
the confusion of unanswered questions.
Forgive us our part in others' pain
and enable us to know your leading
so that we may help and heal them in your name.

(136) Prayer of Thanksgiving

We join in praise of God,
who is our all in all:
who comes to us as whoever meets our need:
mother, father, shepherd, teacher, barrister or friend.

No other god can be to us
the pattern for the time,
the one we long for in our search
for love, for comfort, for company, to share.

And so we thank God from our hearts:
the One who lives, and lives in us,
and cares for us, and meets our needs;
feeding, leading, keeping, caring,
always.

(137) Prayer of Petition

Divine Parent,
you have created our families to be united in purpose,
so that we are not in competition with each other,
but know each other's good,
sharing the moments of rejection and the times of preferment.
Be with all families today, holding them together in love,
sharing successes and failures,
saving them from petty jealousy or presumption,
and granting a measure of your Spirit upon each,
that all may work together to the glory of your kingdom.

(138) Prayer of Dedication or Dismissal

Lord, grant us your eyes, that we may look on the heart,
your will, to enable us to trust,
your ears, that we may be attuned to your leading,
your heart, that we may always have room for you there.

FIFTH SUNDAY IN LENT

(First Sunday of the Passion)

Ezekiel 37.1–14 Psalm 130; Romans 8.6–11; John 11.1–45

OUT OF THE DEPTHS

Presentation

Illustration: deep-sea divers/exploration. 'The Great Deep' was a Hebrew image of the primaeval forces which existed before creation and the sea has remained an image of mystery and fear because of its vastness, unpredictability and power. Draw out how drowning and burial are images we use when we feel overwhelmed by the powers against us, including death itself. God's power enabled Christ to confront the powers of the depths. God's Spirit explores the depths in us, and releases us into life.

(139) Call to Worship

Psalm 130.5–6 *or* John 11.25

(140) Prayer of Adoration and Acknowledgment

Resurrecting Lord,
you promise life to those who trust you,
peace to those who listen to your voice,
a safe passage to those who will be guided by you,
loving acceptance to those who honour your holy name.

As we worship you and bring our prayers of adoration,
be life to us, we pray . . . *Silent, sung or extempore prayer*

Psalm 130 may be read as an acknowledgment of suffering or sin and of our dependence on God's grace. The prayer may be concluded by a declaration of God's love and forgiveness, or by the following Prayer of Petition.

(141) Prayer of Petition

Weeping Lord:
you mourned a friend, yet talked of glory;
share our sorrows, reap our joys.
Compassionate Lord:
you looked in love on those who served you;
be gentle in our grief, and celebrate our hopes.
Dying Lord:
your heart was grieved, yet you spoke of resurrection;
be with us in our dying, then lead us on to life.

(142) Prayer of Thanksgiving

Praise God who heals and rebuilds the body: skin and sinew, flesh
and bone:
We praise you, God of all creation.
Praise God who kindles fire in the heart and stimulates the music of
the mind:
We praise you, God of all creation.
Praise God who stirs the will to compassion and strengthens the
soul to love:
We praise you, God of all creation.
Praise God who breathes into us the life of the Spirit, and through
grace gives us community and hope:
We praise you, God of all creation.

(143) Prayer of Dedication

Lord, we offer you our lives, so often lifeless and dull, or full of
wrong thoughts and actions. Renew us, we pray, that our spirits
may live in your Spirit, dying to self and living for you, showing
your glory in human life.

(144) Prayer of Dismissal

Come, Spirit of God, breathe life into our tired minds,
strength to weakened limbs, sight to clouded eyes,
warmth into hearts that are cold and loveless.
Come, Spirit of God, bring power into ineffective lives,
turn apathy to passion for your cause,
renew, refresh, illuminate our souls,
and send us out, to glorify your name.

SIXTH SUNDAY IN LENT

(Second Sunday of the Passion/Palm Sunday)

Isaiah 50.4–9a; Psalm 118.1–2, 19–29 (or Psalm 31.9–16); Philippians
2.5–11; Matthew 21.1–11 (Matthew 27.11–23, 27–54)

FACING DANGER

Presentation

*Illustration: the story of a person who faced extreme danger and
'won through'. (Sources might be the news, biographies, the lives of
the saints, or the Bible itself.) Talk about the hazards faced and the
qualities/characteristics required to overcome them. How did they
endure or become victorious over fear? What preparations,
disciplines, relationships etc. helped them? What can we learn from
Christ as to how God stands with us and for us in life or ministry?*

(145) Call to worship

Psalm 118.1, 19, 21 *or* Psalm 31.9, 14–16.

(146) Prayer of Adoration

The hour has come! The Lord has need of us!
Open the doors that we may enter with joy!
You are God, we thank you. You are God, we praise you!

The crowds are gathering! Excitement is mounting!
Lead on to God's house in a procession of praise!
You are God, we thank you. You are God, we praise you!

God's word is fulfilled! The Messiah is here!
Come give him the honours that are due to our King!
You are God, we thank you. You are God, we praise you!

Though some doubt and question, and some turn away,
We celebrate Jesus, his hour and his day!
You are God, we thank you. You are God, we praise you!

God's answer to sorrow, to grief and to sin!
Good news for the poor and afraid – he is King!
You are God, we thank you. You are God, we praise you!

(147) Prayer of Acknowledgment

God of grace and mercy, our hearts are weary with the pain of the world, weighed down by the suffering of widows and orphans, burdened by the cries of the hungry, overwhelmed by a sorrow which we have no power to console.
Surround us with your glory: **Save us in your steadfast love.**

Our strength has wasted away through overwork, our energy has been poured out in years of struggle, our hope drained by the relentlessness of corruption, cruelty and greed which robs us of any lasting achievement.
Surround us with your glory: **Save us in your steadfast love.**

We would rather not hear the problems of others anymore. Our eyes cannot bear any more weeping, our ears cannot absorb any more case histories, our minds are baffled and bewildered by the complexities and scale of the misery of the world.
Surround us with your glory: **Save us in your steadfast love.**

Even so, we praise you. Despite all this, we trust you.
In the face of all, we give you our allegiance:
Surround us with your glory: **Save us in your steadfast love.**

For though we are scorned by others, you have not abandoned us.
Though we are criticized by family and friends, you stand by us still.
We may be mocked and find ourselves the butt of jokes,
but you have faith in us, and our future is secure in you.
Surround us with your glory: **Save us in your steadfast love.**

(148) Prayer of Thanksgiving

Creator God, we rest in you, trusting in your strength for our times of weakness, your hope for our moments of despair.
Saviour God, we honour you, grateful for your humble life in our midst, your promise of abiding peace.
Gracious God, we praise you, blessing you for your healing touch, your teaching word, your enlivening presence.

(149) Meditation or Prayer of Dedication

Lord, when I face my accusers –
May I remember the one who emptied himself so completely of pride, that he did not seek to justify his work, his teaching or his name before the throne of power.
May I remember the discipline of his solitude, the dignity of his silence, and the integrity with which he turned the questions on those who sought to wash their hands of responsibility.
May I remember that true authority lies only along the path of hard obedience, generous listening, unstinting offering, outpoured love. And that such devotion is never earned, but given in coin that often lies about despised: the tears of laughter, the sustaining word, the touch of gentleness, and humble praise.

(150) Prayer of Dismissal

Travel with us, God of courage, on our daily road, that we may face the hardships and dangers of the way with your brave compassion and steadfast obedience, and remain faithful to you to the end of our lives.

HOLY WEEK

Isaiah 42.1–9; Psalm 36.5–11; I Corinthians 1.18–31; John 12.20–36

THE SOURCE OF LIFE

Presentation

Illustration: packet of seeds, seed tray filled with soil, small stick for making holes in the soil, water. Plant some of the seeds and discuss how they cannot grow unless they are covered by earth, watered, placed in light/warmth etc. We bury the seed as if it is dead, but in fact we are making it possible for it to grow. So the life of God in Christ seemed to come to an end on Good Friday. His death and burial were real – but not final. God's life is stronger than all our despair, endings and finalities. And this life is the source of all that is life in us.

(151) Call to Worship

Psalm 36.7–9; Isaiah 42.1–4 *or* 5, 8–9.

(152) Prayer of Adoration

O God of all creation, your love for us is vast beyond our imagining, as huge as the over-arching sky, as sure and as solid as a mountain.
Though we may travel into the far reaches of space, or into the depths of the ocean, we shall never travel beyond your care.
So much do you love us; so securely do you keep faith with us:
You are our hope and our trust, O Lord.
Forever we will sing your praise.

O God of all companionship, your love for us is homely and welcoming, your house is a place of feasting and plenty, your presence is a river of delight.
You are the fountain of life and blessing,
of light which allows us to see how much we are loved,
of hope which allows us to praise you more and more:
You are our hope and our trust, O Lord.
Forever we will sing your praise.

O God of all healing, your love for us is a refuge and freedom.
You are the sanctuary into which we can retreat when we are hurt,
and you stand as our Saviour and Advocate against all those who
would harm us.
Remain with us, as we remain in you, so that we may not be driven
astray by weakness or hostility, but instead receive and offer the
forgiveness and mercy on which we depend:
You are our hope and our trust, O Lord.
Forever we will sing your praise.

(153) Prayer of Confession

Loving God, forgive us.
Too often we have preferred the certainties of this world,
the security of human power,
the ingenuity of human cleverness
the safety of small belief:
Loving God, forgive us, for we did not know what we were
doing.

Loving God, shelter us.
In a world without signs, and with so many obstacles to faith
we have needed to know that we were in control,
or at least that everything was under control
according to a plan that we approved:
Loving God, shelter us, so that we can respond to your creative
vision.

Loving God, renew us.
We have condoned the waste of potential, opportunity, life,
the squandering of energy and resources,
the abuse of hope:
Loving God, renew us, so that we can move beyond our
brokenness.

Loving God, command us.
Your call has urged us to a transformation
we have not been willing to undergo,
and has created in us a disquiet that we have muffled with
overwork:
Loving God, command us to take your Good News to all in
need.

(154) Prayer of Thanksgiving

O Living God, source of our life in Christ, all blessing flows from you:
We thank you for the life that is stronger than death.

O Living Christ, you have gone through the door of heaven, taking with you only your tortured flesh and blood, and by this daring of the holy, and in that hidden place, you have made available to us a new covenant, an eternal inheritance, and unlimited grace:
We thank you for the life that is stronger than death.

O Spirit of Life, you allow us to lay aside every weight, and all distractions, so that we can run on: for nothing is more important than the joy that is glimpsed ahead, that shimmer of glory to which Christ ran, with disciplined perseverance, although the cross lay in between:
We thank you for the life that is stronger than death.

(155) Meditation

Here is the seed of life, the hope of glory.
In this hour, this moment, however dull, contained, confined,
however bare, or barren of possibility –
here we can plant the seed.

A small thing, this –
a fragile counter to the might of hatred,
the persistent grudge of resentments carried down
generation to generation, spiting the neighbour, betraying the friend.
Or the complacent sneers of an educated age
which knows too much about everything,
but not enough about what it cannot know.

A tiny thing –
yet set it in the ground of its destruction,
pour it to oblivion in this soil,
and wait the wasted time.
Offer it into mystery, into that which is not ours
to understand or to control.
And see –
the hope reclaimed: the life renewed:
the loss restored: the border breached:
the feeding given.

(156) Prayer of Dedication

Grant us, gracious God,
the courage to walk in your way of costly offering,
where all our life is gratitude
and all our work is generosity
lavished upon your poor.

Grant us, faithful God,
the devotion to walk in your way of light,
where all our words are blessings
and all our deeds are a nourishment
of the body, mind and soul.

Grant us, suffering God
the dedication to walk in your way of the cross,
where all our thought is compassion
and all our prayer an intercession
for your people and your world.

(157) Prayer of Dismissal

Go with God into the joy and pain of the world, knowing that all is known, all is shared, all is given, all is redeemed – through the love of God the Father; the offering of the Son, Jesus Christ our Lord; and the life of the Holy Spirit.

MAUNDY THURSDAY

Exodus 12.1–4 (5–10) 11–14; Psalm 116: 1–2, 12–19;
I Corinthians 11.23–26; John 13.1–17, 31b–35

THE CUP OF SALVATION

Presentation:
Illustration: cups. Make a collection of different cups or drinking containers. Reflect upon them, asking about each: where and when and by whom is it used? What memories or stories are associated with it? From this, draw out the fact that cups 'contain' much that makes us individual, and much that life has offered us, both of joy and of sorrow. How do we bring all this individuality, this personal richness, to our common life? What does the 'one cup' that Christ offers us, contain? As we share it together, how does it challenge us to affirm each other, and value the richness and variety of our life as his Body?

(158) Call to Worship

Psalm 116.12–14 *or* 116.12, 17–19

(159) Prayer of Adoration

Loving God, you have given us this feast
to be enjoyed in your presence,
to be shared with those who love you,
to fill with praise the holiest place,
and to consecrate the humblest home:
We celebrate the feast.

Loving God, you have given us this hour
as a festival of prayer that has been heard,
as a deepening of our love for one another,
as a rejoicing with you, for you enjoy our company,
and as a moment of challenge, commitment and change:
We celebrate the feast.

(160) Prayer of Confession

a prayer for two voices

Voice 1: 'Precious in the sight of the Lord is the death of his faithful ones . . .'

Voice 2: But we have been most unwilling to die.

Voice 1: O God of grace, you call us to offer ourselves in surrender, honesty, humility, brokenness,

Voice 2: But we have preferred a superficial healing, a temporary victory, an inadequate offering, second-best praise.

Voice 1: O God of grace, you have delivered us from death, loosed the bonds which held us, pushed back the forces which threatened to overwhelm us,

Voice 2: But we have been reluctant to complete what has been begun. We have quailed at the cost to our pride, we have closed our eyes to the truth. We have refused to know.

Voice 1: Yet now is the moment of your judgment. Now is all power and wisdom gathered into your hands as you kneel to serve our needs.

Voice 2: Now is all truth given as your life is given, revealing the reality of our faith, our communion and our love.

(161) Prayer of Thanksgiving

To remember Jesus, to keep his memory alive in our midst, and to obey his command:
We celebrate the feast.

To give thanks to you, O God, to offer the gratitude and praise which is our duty and our joy:
We celebrate the feast.

To honour your promises, and our own, to open our hearts and our community to your grace, and to seek your healing:
We celebrate the feast.

To lift again the cup of our salvation, in which is gathered all that you have done for us, and all that we share in your name, with those here, and with those who have gone before us:
We celebrate the feast.

To hold what we have received –
that the Lord Jesus took bread, gave thanks, broke it, and shared it
with his friends –
and to live in this way, proclaiming his death until he comes:
We celebrate the feast.

(162) Prayer of Dedication

At the moment of Passover,
when the power of death is at our door, but does not enter:
We trust in you alone.
As you strip yourself of pride and dignity,
and kneel in naked humility to wash our feet,
revealing, by your generosity, our pettiness and evil:
We trust in you alone.
As we are cleansed by your forgiveness,
healed by your word, made noble by your touch,
and lovely in your sight:
We trust in you alone.
As we surrender our lives for each other,
claiming in faith your victory,
even while we live with bitterness, hardship and poverty:
We trust in you alone.

(163) Prayer of Dismissal

Uphold us, God of compassion,
as we wait with you through the long night of testing and betrayal,
that we may learn your patience and receive your peace.

GOOD FRIDAY

Isaiah 52.13–53.12; Psalm 22; Hebrews 10.16–25
(or Hebrews 4.14–16; 5.7–9); John 18.1–19.42
John 19.17–30 or 17–42 could be read if a shorter gospel is required.

THE DEATH OF OUR HOPE

Presentation

Illustration: the cross of our hope. Prepare a large, freestanding cross. List the hopes that we might have for ourselves, our families and friends, our community, our world, writing them down on pieces of card which are then attached to the cross. Ask: what are the realities which make it hard to sustain these hopes? What are the realities which kill our hope? How can we support each other in situations where all hope seems gone? Do we sometimes need to 'go down into the depths' with others, to a point where, despite our faith, reality seems irredeemable? How can the crucified Christ guide us to – and through – such places?

(164) Call to Worship

Psalm 22.1–5 *or* Isaiah 53.1, 6.

(165) Prayer of Adoration

Lord of eternity,
you are all holiness and grace.
Yours is the ultimate sovereignty and power.
We know you will hear us and help us and save us
from the death of the heart,
the death of the spirit
and the death of our hope:
We praise you.

(166) Prayer of Confession

Forgive us, Lord Jesus, for the suffering you receive at our hands:
that we despise your sacrificial life, and are not attracted to your way;
that we lay upon you all our sickness, pain and grief,
and are not grateful for your saving help.
Silence.

Lord, in your mercy: **Hear our prayer.**

Forgive us, Lord Jesus, that we refuse to hear your voice:
that we reject your call to a new commitment,
and jump to false conclusions about the judgment of God;
that we consider you to be less than ourselves
mocking your faith, sneering at your ideals,
and accusing you of collusion with the forces of wealth and power.
Silence.

Lord, in your mercy: **Hear our prayer.**

Forgive us, Lord Jesus, that we deny respect to your humanity:
encircling you as an enemy, surrounding you with hatred and
    threats;
that we laugh at your nakedness, pierce you, expose you, and
    delight
when we find you abandoned and afraid.
Silence.

Lord, in your mercy: **Hear our prayer.**

Forgive us, Lord Jesus, that we fail to understand your humility:
your patient learning through obedience,
your silence before those who would destroy you,
your outpouring of your soul to death,
your reliance on God alone.
Silence.

Lord, in your mercy: **Hear our prayer.**

Forgive us, Lord Jesus, that we belittle the mystery of your death:
that we too easily avoid your weakness, ignore your temptations,
deny your frailty, evade your cross.
Silence.

Lord, in your mercy: **Hear our prayer.**

(167) Prayer of Thanksgiving

Thank you, God of all grace, that your Son did not forego the cross,
but with it, carried our burden, and on its wide-stretched arms
made himself an offering for our wrong.

Thank you, God of all power, that your Son did not avoid the cross,
but on it made his intercession for the life we have corrupted
and the joy that we have wasted and abused.

Thank you, God of all hope, that your Son did not escape the cross, but that through his offering of a pain and grief already won by love, we are released for healing, and in love sent out to all the world.

(168) Prayer of Petition

O Christ the Way, as you have laid down life for us
taking the road of death to its final end:
stay with us in grief, that we may know your companion word
in emptiness and absence.

O Christ the Door, open for us the gateway you have made
through the concealing curtain:
that living in your presence we may know ourselves transformed
as children of your labour and your joy.

O Christ the Truth, stand with us in the tomb
where we would declare your light and peace,
not in shallow comfort nor defiance, but as a living of your life
claimed back from fear, and radiant with your glory.

(169) Prayer of Dedication

For the light that we seek beyond the wall,
Lord we pray: **Hear us and lead us on.**
For the love that we seek beyond estrangement, hatred, loneliness,
Lord, we pray: **Hear us and lead us on.**
For the peace that we seek beyond the pain and weariness which
    drag us down,
Lord, we pray: **Hear us and lead us on.**
For the justice that we seek beyond poverty and oppression,
Lord, we pray: **Hear us and lead us on.**
For the faith that we seek beyond confusion, betrayal and doubt,
Lord, we pray: **Hear us and lead us on.**
For the communion that we seek beyond division, violence, war,
Lord, we pray: **Hear us and lead us on.**
For the hope we seek beyond the death of all our hopes,
Lord, we pray: **Hear us and lead us on.**

(170) Prayer of Dismissal

Strengthen us, God of life,
as we wait with you through the long night of desolation and sorrow,
that we may learn your silence and receive your shelter in our grief.

HOLY SATURDAY

Job 14.1–14 (or Lamentations 3.1–9, 19–24); Psalm 31.1–4, 15–16;
I Peter 4.1–8; Matthew 27.57–66 (or John 19.38–42)

INTO GOD'S HANDS

Presentation
Illustration: trustworthy hands. List or illustrate different ways in which we use our hands to help, support, care for or heal one another. Show how we trust other people to do these things for us when we cannot do them for ourselves because we are too young, old, ill, hampered etc. In what ways do we 'put ourselves in the hands of others?' Draw the link between this and the ways in which God helps, supports, cares for and heals us. This being so, what does it mean to pray 'Into thy hands, O Lord, I commit my spirit?'

(171) Call to Worship

Psalm 31.1–4 (or 1–5); *or* Job 14.13–14.

(172) Prayer of Adoration and Acknowledgment

O God of hope, we come to you,
although we have lost our peace:
Gone is our glory and our expectation from the Lord.
O God of life, we come to you,
although we feel as if we are already dead:
We are like failing waters, like a dried up stream.
O God of light, we come to you,
bringing our flaws, our failings and our woes:
We are like those who live in the valley of shadow.
O God of love, we come to you,
even though we do not sense your tenderness:
It is as though we have been driven far from your sight.
O God of forgiveness, we come to you,
even though our cares press upon us like a judgment:
We need a place in which to hide.
O God of renewal, we come to you,
even though we are convinced that nothing will change:
Evil imprisons us;
we know our sin, and our need of grace.

(173) Prayer of Petition

Can I live beyond this death?
There is night but no morning:
Take courage, for God is faithful.

Can I live beyond this death?
A hand has been turned against me, marking me down.
I am hungry, but can eat only grave and sand:
Take courage, for God is generous.

Can I live beyond this death?
I am hemmed in by trouble, besieged by bitterness.
Prayer is shut out, the way is blocked, the path made crooked;
I have been ambushed, diverted from the true way, torn into pieces:
Take courage, for God is a guiding vision.

Can I live beyond this death?
Like a broken vessel, I am ignored and unthought of,
except as beyond redemption:
Take courage, for God is our hope.

What hope can there be for humanity?
What hope can there be for me? For us?
Can I live beyond this death?
Silence

(174) Thanksgiving

Faithful God, you have never ceased to love us.
You have never turned your ear from our cry or failed to meet our
need:
We praise you.
Eternal God, there are no boundaries to your compassion.
You have never refused your grace or hesitated to reach out to
those in pain:
We praise you.
Mysterious God, we place our trust in your mercy even as we rage
in protest at the injustice of the world. We believe that you will
keep faith with us, even though we meet only your silence:
We praise you.

(175) Meditation

We offer our faith like spices brought for the dead,
to be cast upon a body, to be buried with our hope.
We offer our attention in silence,
numbed by sacrifice and solitude,
hemmed in by decay and corruption,
guarded by fear.
We offer our love like women laying out a corpse,
knowing that the power of love lies,
not in any ability to defy death,
but in our willingness to accept it as real.
As real, I say, but not as truth,
despite the mocking laughter.

(176) Prayer of Dedication

O Living God, there is hope for the tree, because growth and the
power of growth are eternal. Hope is renewed every morning,
For we trust you: **And our times are in your hand.**

There is hope in our covenant with you, that at a time of your
choosing you will remember us and our trouble. You are our
portion. We are bound by an everlasting love.
For we trust you: **And our times are in your hand.**

There is hope in our patience and your faithfulness. For there is no
end to your love and your mercy, and all the days that we serve you
we will wait, until we are released from our suffering.
For we trust you: **And our times are in your hand.**

There is hope in your power, for you help us stand amidst turmoil,
and you are our defence against the enemy, so that we are not
confused or overcome. You have seen, you have heard, you will
save us.
For we trust you: **And our times are in your hand.**

*O Living God, let your life renew our confidence, so that we can
leave our future in your keeping. Let your love renew our hope, so
that we may take courage to wait for your hour.
For we trust you: **And our times are in your hand.**

*This paragraph may be used, or repeated, as a prayer of
dismissal.*

EASTER DAY

Acts 10.34–43 (or Jeremiah 31.1–6); Psalm 118.1–2, 14–24;
Colossians 3.1–4 (or Acts 10.34–43); John 20.1–18
(or Matthew 28.1–10)

LIFE BEYOND HOPE

Presentation

Illustration: the Good News Cross. [Prior to the service, take the prayers of hope from the cross (see presentation for Good Friday) and place in an offering plate on the communion table.] Distribute pieces of card (perhaps appropriately decorated) throughout the congregation, and invite people to write on them a positive statement of Easter Good News (e.g. 'God gives healing' or 'Love is stronger than death'). Reflect how the resurrection of Jesus points us to a hope beyond the life we know, even a life beyond our hopes. Collect the cards and pin all or some to the cross. At the end of the service, invite children to take them down and distribute them amongst the congregation at random, perhaps with a flower as a symbol of joy and healing.

(177) Call to Worship

Psalm 118.1–2 *or* 21–24; *or* Jeremiah 31.2–3.

(178) Prayer of Adoration

O God of all creation, for the life which springs up, beyond our
dreams or our deserving: **We adore you. Alleluia!**
O God of saving power, for the love that is stronger than
destruction or the grave: **We adore you. Alleluia!**
O God of healing mercy, for the grace that is given to bring all
things into harmony in Christ: **We praise your holy name.
Alleluia!**

(179) Prayer of Thanksgiving

We have fled from the sword and found grace in the wilderness.
We have been wearied by our burdens,
but you have refreshed us with living water:
O God of life, we praise you.

We have felt betrayed by those we loved,
but you have strengthened us through your faithfulness.
We have been ruined and broken down,
but you are building us again to your glory:
O God of life, we praise you.

We have been soiled and stained by sin,
but you are making us holy and pure.
We have been struck down by grief,
but you have turned mourning into joy:
O God of life, we praise you.

We have been withered and barren,
but in your grace we are bearing new fruit,
You have loved us with an everlasting love,
You have continued your faithfulness towards us:
O God of life, we praise you.

(180) Meditation

We came seeking the dead,
   but it was not death that terrified us in the garden,
   but a life we could not understand.
We came feeling our grief,
   but it was not sorrow that wrung our hearts,
   but a love which would not let us hold on
   to what was so precious.
We came seeing an end,
   but it was not finality that cast a wall across our sight,
   but a new beginning we had never imagined.
We came expecting nothing,
   but it was not memory which sang us into wonder and joy,
   but an answer, a marvel, a glory.

(181) Prayer of Dedication

Let us worship our God in doing justice,
for our God has no favourites, and calls us to do what is right.
Come, let us go up to Zion:
Let us worship the Lord our God. Alleluia!

Let us worship our God in making peace,
for our God is healing the nations.
and calls us to be agents of reconciliation.
Come, let us go up to Zion:
Let us worship the Lord our God. Alleluia!

Let us worship our God in the Spirit,
for our God is renewing the church, and calls us to service and
    praise.
Come, let us go up to Zion:
Let us worship the Lord our God. Alleluia!

Let us worship our God in truth,
for our God is Judge of the living and the dead, and calls us to
    wisdom and knowledge.
Come, let us go up to Zion:
Let us worship the Lord our God. Alleluia!

(182) Prayer of Dismissal

Let us live in the joy and peace of the risen Christ.
Let us work in confidence, trusting in the victory of his
    resurrection.
Let us look for his coming as one who gives life beyond our hope.

SECOND SUNDAY OF EASTER

Exodus 14.10–31; 15.20–21; Acts 2.14a, 22–32; Psalm 16; I Peter 1.3–9; John 20.19–31

WE ARE ALL WITNESSES

Presentation

Illustration: a mock 'trial' of a cat who is accused of injuring a mouse. Set up a 'court' with judge, counsel, clerks etc. and the congregation as the jury. Call witnesses for the prosecution and defence, to demonstrate in simple terms the different kinds of evidence available: circumstantial (the cat seen in the neighbourhood where the injured mouse was found); character (the cat known to hate the mouse); and eye-witness (the cat seen to attack the mouse). Draw out the value of eye-witness evidence, and ask: how valuable is our witness to Jesus as one who gives life? Is it circumstantial (we are sometimes seen going to church); of character (we are agreed to be good people); or eye-witness (we know he has given us new life and we are eager to share that life with others).

(183) Call to Worship

Psalm 16.5–6, 11; *or* I Peter 1.3.

(184) Prayer of Adoration

Blessed be God, Father of mercy, giver of life and hope:
We will rejoice in your love.
Blessed be God, Saviour and Christ, giver of freedom and peace:
We will rejoice in your love.
Blessed be God, Holy compassion, Spirit of glory and grace:
We will rejoice in your love.

(185) Prayer of Acknowledgment

When the German theologian Jürgen Moltmann visited Auschwitz, he performed the customary act of kneeling on the ground and running the bone-brittle earth through his fingers. As he did so, he claimed that for God to be vindicated, the children of Auschwitz must be raised: this is the meaning of resurrection. This conviction lies behind the words of assurance at the end of this prayer.

When disaster comes
and nothing makes sense
and nothing feels right,
we feel abandoned by you, O God,
and cry to you to prove yourself a God of love.

When children cry
and their cries are not heard
and they die from neglect,
we feel abandoned by you, O God,
and cry to you to prove yourself a God of love.

When peace breaks down
and lives are maimed
by bombs and tanks and mines,
we feel abandoned by you, O God,
and cry to you to prove yourself a God of love.

When Jesus died
and was placed in the tomb –
the hope of all the earth destroyed –
we felt abandoned by you, O God,
and cried to you to prove yourself a God of love.
Silence.

And then we heard the words of grace: Jesus is raised.
These children will rise. Death is not the final word.
God is love.

(186) Prayer of Thanksgiving

Thank you, gracious Christ, for the peace which steps gently into
the midst of our fear, even when we bar the door against you; for
the peace which speaks to our need from the costly depths of your
own loving; for the peace which sends us out in your name, as
wounded healers, forgiven sinners, children reborn, outcasts raised
from the dead.

(187) Prayer of Dedication

This prayer can be shared between several voices. Silence could be kept between each section.

I am a witness that Jesus is alive,
bringing broken people back to life.
This Jesus God raised up; he is alive:
And of that we are all the witnesses.

I am a witness that Jesus is alive
hearing the cries of the hungry on our streets.
This Jesus God raised up; he is alive:
And of that we are all the witnesses.

I am a witness that Jesus is alive
speaking out against injustice and oppression.
This Jesus God raised up; he is alive:
And of that we are all the witnesses.

I am a witness that Jesus is alive
carrying the pain of caring.
This Jesus God raised up; he is alive:
And of that we are all the witnesses.

I am a witness that Jesus is alive
in the hearts of those who put their trust in him.
This Jesus God raised up; he is alive:
And of that we are all the witnesses.

(188) Prayer of Dismissal

Let us go out from this place
And bear witness to the living Christ in our world:
**Let us go out in his living joy,
for we have seen his glory!**

THIRD SUNDAY OF EASTER

Acts 2.14a, 36–41; Psalm 116.1–4, 12–19; I Peter 1.17–23;
Luke 24.13–35

INTO THE FUTURE

Presentation

Illustration: a 'time-machine' (simply constructed from a chair, a dial and some means of showing the date). Send a volunteer 'forward in time' by a year, ten years, twenty years, as appropriate. What sort of world do we find? Draw out peoples' ideas on this, and reflect upon what this reveals of our hopes and fears for the future. Do we have a sense of God leading us into the future? What difference does it make to our hopes and our fears if we are travelling into the future with the risen Christ?

(189) Call to Worship

Psalm 116.1–2, 14; *or* I Peter 1.23; *or the following:*

Voice 1: Is it true the Lord is risen and has vanished from the tomb?
Voice 2: Is it true the Lord is risen and has been seen alive?
It is true: the Lord is risen! We have met him on the way and he has turned our sorrow into the dance of life.

(190) Prayer of Adoration

O God of life, you are the one who comes to us out of the mystery;
who walks with us, unrecognized, as the stranger on our road;
who speaks to our bewilderment and grief, our need for company
and compassion:
We adore you.

(191) Meditation or Prayer of Acknowledgment

Psalm 116 may be read, followed by silence, then the following:

When we call on God there is no sound;
there are no words to hear in answer.
Only stillness and quiet, peace and poise –
and the knowledge that God is good,
and we are loved, and all shall be well in God's good time.

(192) Prayer of Thanksgiving

We thank you, God of life, for the impartial care with which you
watch over us, calling us into deeper reverence and awe.
We thank you, Saviour Christ, for the liberating power of your
dying and rising again, which renews us in freedom and hope.
We thank you, encouraging Spirit, for the strength to obey and the
humility to learn, so that our words and deeds are purified.
We thank you, creative God, that you hold our past in your mercy,
our present in your compassion, our future in your desire.

(193) Prayer of Petition or Dedication

Lord God, you went before the Israelites
in a pillar of cloud and a pillar of fire,
leading them from slavery to freedom:
Lead us, your travelling people, in the paths that lead to life.

Lord God, you walked with your disciples
along the Emmaus Road,
leading them from grief to exuberant hope:
Lead us, your travelling people, in the paths that lead to life.

Lord God, you met your apostles at Pentecost
with rushing wind and visionary tongues of flame,
leading them to dance and sing for joy:
Lead us, your travelling people, in the paths that lead to life.

Lord God, our guide, our hope, our dance:
Lead us, your travelling people, in the paths that lead to life.

(194) Prayer of Dismissal

When we set out upon a journey, there are choices to be made –
what to take and what to leave behind. We may be fearful of the
road and where it all will end – or travel hopefully.
On our journey to the future let us choose to follow Christ; and
though fearful, let us trust that he will meet us on the way, and set
our hearts on fire with hope and joy and life and good news to tell
to all.

FOURTH SUNDAY OF EASTER

Acts 2.42–47; Psalm 23; I Peter 2.19–25; John 10.1–10

THE GOOD SHEPHERD

Presentation

Illustration: a sheepfold. Construct a 'sheepfold' with a circle of chairs, perhaps draped with blankets. Leave a narrow gap as the entrance. Demonstrate how the shepherd would himself sleep across this gap to prevent sheep straying or predators entering, thus becoming the 'door' or the 'gate' of the sheep. What are the qualities of the good shepherd as expounded by John's Gospel? How do we see these qualities lived out by Christ? Or by our own Christian leaders? If we are the 'sheep' how should we respond to our shepherds?

(195) Call to Worship

Psalm 23.1–2; Psalm 100.1–3; *or* I Peter 2.21, 25.

(196) Prayer of Adoration

Let us praise the Lord who is a great God –
   the God who brought us to birth,
    and who cares for us as a shepherd cares for the sheep.
Let us praise the Lord whose Son Jesus Christ is the Good Shepherd
   who came to rescue us,
    and lead us out into the warmth of the sun.
Let us praise the Lord who breathes the Holy Spirit upon us
   to convince us in our bones that the Lord is God
    and we are his people, the sheep of his pasture.
Let us praise the Lord, the source and word and breath of life,
   the one true shepherd of the sheep.

(197) Prayer of Confession and Thanksgiving

Let us return to the One who is shepherd and guardian of our souls:
Let us return to God.
For we have lacked endurance in the face of suffering; we have been too concerned for our rights and impatient of the needs of others; we have rebelled against injustice with vengeful bitterness; we have criticized and dealt out blame, quick to vent our feelings, slow to heed the demands of truth. Loving God, forgive us:

Loving Shepherd, guide us in your way of demanding compassion, so that we may learn to see our sufferings in the light of your own path through death to resurrection.
Silence.

We give thanks that we may bear the burdens of others for their blessing and healing; that through our offering they may die to wrong-doing and live for the right; that through our love they may discover your freedom:
Let us return to the One who is shepherd and guardian of our souls. Let us return to God.

(198) Meditation

This meditation translates John 10.1–10 into an alternative image. It can be used to follow the Gospel reading, or to provoke discussion on the nature and purpose of Christian leadership. It could also form the basis for mime.

There was once a bad mother who kept her children locked in a room. She told the neighbours it was to keep them safe, but really it was to make them work. From dawn until dusk they sewed slippers for the factory and had nothing to eat except a bowl of soup at night. All day the mother would stand in the doorway, watching the work, so none could escape, paying them nothing, but keeping all the profits for herself. She grew rich and fat, while her children grew thin and pale. And the children lived in fear of the bad mother – for they knew in their bones she was bad.

Until one day the bad mother was ill through over-eating and was taken to hospital. A neighbour came and stood in the doorway of the room where the children worked. She was very angry – for the children were thin and pale. 'I will be a good mother,' she said, 'I will not make you work for my own profit – but I will take you out into the sunshine to play.' She called the children by their names which they had almost forgotten, and they followed the good mother out into the fresh air. And they laughed and they played and they danced with delight, and they followed the good mother wherever she went – for they knew in their bones she was good.

(199) Prayer of Petition or Dedication

O Christ, the Good Shepherd,
you seek us when we are lost, gathering us in your arms,
so that we can find our safety in your presence:
Grant us no rest until we find our rest in you.

O Christ, the Gate for the sheep,
you stand by the door and call us by name,
guiding us out to open pasture:
Grant that we may follow you and none other.

O Christ, the Good Shepherd,
you put your life on the line for the sheep
dying that they might live – and live abundantly:
**Grant that we may seek the fullness which you offer –
for ourselves and for one another,
until your kingdom come.**

(200) Prayer of Thanksgiving

*This litany is based on Psalm 23. You may need to explain to
children the idea of knowing something 'in our bones'. Young
children can be taught the response, perhaps with the help of simple
actions:*
And I know (*touch the temple*) in my bones (*clasp the fingers of
one hand in the other*) he is good (*thumbs up!*)

The Lord is my shepherd, he keeps me calm and safe:
And I know in my bones he is good.
He rescues me from despair, and brings me out into the sun:
And I know in my bones he is good.
Even in times of trouble I need not shake with fear:
For I know in my bones he is good.
He shames those who hate me with his kindness, and I leap for joy:
And I know in my bones he is good.
Surely the world is full of goodness,
so I shall follow the Good Shepherd wherever he leads:
For I know in my bones he is good.

(201) Prayer of Dismissal

May the Good Shepherd lead us through the pastures of the world,
feeding us with his life and strengthening us with his love.

FIFTH SUNDAY OF EASTER

Acts 7.55–60; Psalm 31.1–5, 15–16; I Peter 2.2–10; John 14.1–14

THE TOWER

Presentation

Illustration: towers of various kinds. Make a list of the different towers people have known. (The 'tower' might be largely symbolic, such as a monument or a cairn.) Draw out the different reasons why towers have been constructed: for refuge, defence, containment, guidance, status, ambition, display, decoration, remembrance. What does it mean to have God as our tower, our castle, our stronghold? How is God a 'defence' for us? And if we wish to build a tower to reveal our faith, what kind of structure might it be? A huge wayside cross? A prayer cairn? A bell-tower?

(202) Call to Worship

Psalm 31.1–2 *or* 14–16; I Peter 2.4–5; John 14.1; *or the following:*

Christ is a tower of strength. In times of trouble, he is solid as a rock:
Therefore, we need not be afraid; but may come out into the open.

(203) Prayer of Adoration

Glory to God who has opened the heavens so that we may glimpse a vision of Jesus, and the future glory in which he has prepared for us a home: **Glory to God!**
Glory to God who has shown us in our Saviour a way of generosity which will take us into the very depths of love: **Glory to God!**
Glory to God who lives in us as we live in light, so that our need may be satisfied by grace, and our word and work may carry the authority of hope: **Glory to God!**

(204) Prayer of Petition or Acknowledgment

Protect us, O God, and rescue us:
Make us safe in your love.
Listen to us, and listen now:
Make us safe in your love.

Be for us a rock to hide in, a castle where we will feel secure:
Make us safe in your love.
You are our rock, O God, and a strong defence:
Make us safe in your love.
Set us free when we are trapped:
Make us safe in your love.
Only you can shelter us, for you have rescued us before:
We shall be safe in your love.

(205) Prayer of Thanksgiving

We come to you in gladness, God of peace: for you have brought
us through death to new birth, from a way of destruction to a path
of hope:
We have tasted the sweetness of your grace.

We come to you in praise, God of hope: for you have brought us
from fear to love, from a nightmare to your vision of life for all
people:
We have tasted the sweetness of your grace.

We come to you in joy, God of life: for you have brought us from
despair to a new beginning, where holy hearts will build justice
throughout the land:
We have tasted the sweetness of your grace.

(206) Meditation

*Each member of the congregation could receive a rounded pebble as
a visual aid during the reflection. Afterwards, these could be built
into a cairn, perhaps as part of a sharing of concerns for prayer.
Alternatively, appropriate slides could be shown for each paragraph
of the meditation.*

I am a stone, a pebble, grained and scarred
and yet smoothed by the currents of time.

I am a stone, a pebble, battered and tired
by the ebb and flow of the daily tide.

I am a stone, a pebble, plain and small;
one amongst so many thousands on this vast sea of a beach.

I am a stone, a pebble, dull and worn,
yet in living water I sparkle: I am beautiful.

I am a stone, a pebble, alone not strong,
yet set in a wall I can bear much weight.

We are stones and pebbles – grained and tired, plain and worn,
yet together we are destined as the church of Christ
to strengthen beauty for the healing of the world.

(207) Prayer of Dismissal

God is building us, as living stones, into a house of prayer:
We will live in trust.
God is forming us, in tender compassion, into a community of
service to others:
We will live in love.
God is creating us, a holy people, into a temple of sacrifice and
glory:
We will live in praise.

SIXTH SUNDAY OF EASTER

Acts 17.22–31; Psalm 66.8–20; 1 Peter 3.13–22; John 14.15–21

ANONYMOUS

Presentation
Illustration: Items of 'anonymous' work (newspaper editorials, letters to the editor, hymns, poems, nursery rhymes, etc. including a 'love letter' written out on a large sheet of paper, but with the signature blocked out). Discuss how we feel about reading something where we do not know the author. Does knowing/not knowing make a difference? How do we feel if the subject matter is disagreeable, even nasty? Knowing the author/sender increases our trust in the work, and allows us to respond. Reflect on how God has become known in Christ, but also remains mysterious and, in one sense, forever unknown, because forever beyond us.

(208) Call to Worship

Psalm 66.8–9, 20, *or* 13–14, 16; *or* John 14.18–19.

(209) Prayer of Adoration

In you we live and move
and all we are is known to you –
the depths of fear and the heights of hope
and the endlessness of our need for love:
Loving God, we adore you.

In you is space and breadth and room
for each of us to be ourselves –
to stretch and breathe, to laugh and weep
and sound the songs we long to sing:
Loving God, we adore you.

In you is time and strength to wait
for each of us to dare to dream and trust our hope
that you are love which does not end –
but ever holds us safe and close:
Loving God, we adore you.

In you we find ourselves fulfilled –
the unknown God, unseen, unnamed,
the great I AM who is, for us,
the word of life, made flesh, come true:
Loving God, we adore you.

(210) Prayer of Confession

For fearing the unknown and failing to search and seek after truth:
Good Lord, forgive us.
For fearing the faith of others and limiting your love to people like
   us:
Good Lord, forgive us.
For being content with the outward forms of religion and being
   afraid to change for good:
Good Lord, forgive us.
For placing our trust in money and status and failing to worship in
   openness and trust:
Good Lord, forgive us.
Silence.

The Lord is good and quick to forgive. Let us trust in his word and
make a new start, to the glory of God.

Prayers of Thanksgiving

(211)

God of grace, we rest in you. Though we have feared you in the
unknown, and have been daunted by your silence, yet you have
brought us through fire and water into a spacious place where we
are consoled by your presence, comforted by your strength and
counselled by your truth. You have given us life again, and we
praise you, God of love and grace.

(212)

Minister: Come and hear what the Lord has done,
            The unknown God, unseen, unnamed.
Voice 1:   He has brought into being all that is –
Voice 2:   All peoples and all nations –
Voice 3:   And time and space for all to live,
Voice 4:   And room to search for truth and love:
We have heard and now we believe.

Minister:	Come and hear what the Lord has done
	The unknown God, unseen, unnamed –
Voice 1:	He has shown his face in Jesus Christ –
Voice 2:	A man who spoke and danced,
Voice 3:	A man who wept and smiled,
Voice 4:	A man who brings new life from grief and death:

We have heard and now we believe.

Minister:	Come and hear what the Lord has done
	The unknown God, unseen, unnamed –
Voice 1:	He has breathed a Holy Spirit –
Voice 2:	A spirit of wisdom and strength,
Voice 3:	A spirit of freedom and life,
Voice 4:	A spirit who lifts our hearts to sing:

We have heard and now we believe.

(213) Prayer of Dismissal

Go in the love of God who will keep you through any adversity.
Go in the peace of Christ who will sustain you when you are
trampled by others.
Go in the light of the Spirit who will guide you through the
entanglements of sin.
That the glory of God may be revealed in you, this day and forever.

ASCENSION DAY

Acts 1.1–11; Psalm 47 (or Psalm 93, or Psalm 110);
Ephesians 1.15–23; Luke 24.44–53

THE POWER AND THE GLORY

Presentation
Illustration: 'Crown Jewels' – orb, sceptre, crown, sword. Show pictures of the real ones, or improvise your own with gold card, glittery materials, silver paper etc. What kind of power do these items symbolize? What ideal characteristics or qualities do they represent? How is the power of God similar to – or different from – this earthly kingship? What might be the 'crown jewels' of the kingdom of God? Is the word 'power' even appropriate at all to describe the nature of God's rule?

(214) Call to Worship

Psalm 47.5–7; Psalm 93.1–2; *or* Ephesians 1.15–17.

(215) Prayer of Adoration

Sovereign God, creator of the universe, foundation of all strength,
source of all life, enthroned in majesty and splendour:
We adore you.

Glorious God, light of the world and teacher of holiness, unshaken
in truth and ancient wisdom:
We adore you.

Marvellous God, steadfast love, maker of justice and minister of
peace, drawing all peoples and all creation into hope:
We adore you.

(216) Prayer of Confession

Forgive us, God of all love, that we have not obeyed your call to
service, nor encouraged each other in your praise. We have not
acknowledged your rule and reign in every area of our lives, nor
have we radiated your glory:
Forgive us, God of glory.

Forgive us, God of all peace, that too often we have been
overwhelmed by the flood of evil and wrongdoing which covers the
world. We have listened to the thunder of power and the roar of
violence and hatred. We have drowned in the waters of cynicism
and despair:
Forgive us, God of glory.

(217) Prayer of Thanksgiving

All power belongs to you, living God.
Yours is the kingdom beyond all the nations of the earth.
Yours is a court where all are welcome,
where all are heard, where justice is done,
and those who are oppressed go free:
Living God, we praise your holy name.

All power belongs to you, holy God.
Yours is a dominion beyond the reach of human spite.
Yours is a peace in which all are held,
where all are healed, where right is recognized,
and those who have done right receive their due reward:
Holy God, we praise your holy name.

All power belongs to you, saving God.
Yours is a mercy beyond our understanding.
Yours is a truth before which all are judged,
in which all are purified, where corruption and malice are burned
    out,
and the forces of hatred and violence are broken forever:
Saving God, we praise your holy name.

(218) Prayer of Petition

Ascended Jesus, as we wait for you,
stay with us, share with us, feed us with your life,
and teach us the nature of your kingdom.

Ascended Jesus, as we wait for you,
sing with us, laugh with us, fill us with your joy,
and show us how all things are fulfilled in you.

Ascended Jesus, as we wait for you,
serve with us, weep with us, open our hearts with your love,
and strengthen us in the patience of faith.

Ascended Jesus, as we wait for you,
gaze with us, dream with us, prepare us for your coming,
and draw us deeper into gratitude and praise.

(219) Prayer of Dedication

Father God, remembering all that you have provided for us,
and giving thanks for your guidance, your forgiveness
and your care: we will witness to your love:
We will declare your glory.

Saviour Jesus, remembering all that you have suffered for us,
and giving thanks for your ministry, your death,
and your rising again, we will witness to your love:
We will declare your glory.

Holy Spirit, remembering all that you have taught us,
and giving thanks for your strength, your encouragement,
and your faith in us, we will witness to your love:
We will declare your glory.

Generous God, Maker, Redeemer and Friend,
remembering how you have called us into hope,
and giving thanks for the riches of our inheritance and the security
of your promises, we will witness to your love:
We will declare your glory.

(220) Prayer of Dismissal

In the power of God who raised Jesus from death,
in the justice of God who is judge of the living and the dead,
and in the mercy of God who has forgiven and healed us:
go into the world as witnesses to the One who is all glory
and who reigns in love forever.

SEVENTH SUNDAY OF EASTER

Acts 1.6–14; Psalm 68.1–10, 32–35; I Peter 4.12–14; 5.6–11;
John 17.1–11

HEARTS OF FLESH, NOT STONE

Presentation

*Illustration: a pin-cushion and a stone. Demonstrate the essential
difference between the two, that one is soft and squishy, the other
hard and unresponsive. Show too, how the pin-cushion, being
padded, can absorb and hold the pins. What does it mean to have a
heart like a stone? Or a heart like a pin-cushion? Does this help us
understand what is meant by a 'a heart of flesh'?*

(221) Call to Worship

Psalm 68.3–4, *or* 32–35; *or* Acts 1.10–11; *or* I Peter 4.12–13;
*or the following, which can be chanted with the congregation
clapping time and repeating each phrase after the leader.*

Let God's people rejoice! Let us sing before God!
Let us sing out for joy! Sing our praises to God!
Sing a song of God's power! For our God is the Lord!

(222) Prayer of Adoration

O wild and wonderful God,
you marched with your people through the wilderness,
turning the desert into a garden,
changing a barren landscape into a place of plenty,
with water and bread and meat provided for all.
Come, wild and wonderful God:
Turn our hearts towards you once more.

O wild and wonderful God,
you call us into your holy presence,
where we are challenged by your pure love,
taught by your word of life,
transformed by your energy of grace.
Come, wild and wonderful God:
Turn our hearts towards you once more.

(223) Prayer of Confession

God of compassion, receive into your forgiving grace all that is less than love in our world – look upon us with mercy:
Hear our prayer.

God of grace, turning the sufferings of your Son into a glory of redeeming love – look upon us with mercy:
Hear our prayer.

God of love, transforming the struggles of our lives into a way in which we bring peace to others – look upon us with mercy:
Hear our prayer.

God of peace, renewing the fabric of society through our generosity to become a community of justice – look upon us with mercy:
Hear our prayer.

God of justice, calling your church through sacrifice to witness to the truth of your gospel – look upon us with mercy:
Hear our prayer.

God of holiness, receive into your forgiving grace all that we have done amiss . . .
Silence.

Look upon us with mercy:
Hear our prayer.

(224) Prayer of Thanksgiving

Read the Epistle in short sections, e.g. I Peter 4.12–14; 5.6; 5.7; 5.8–9; 5.10–11, each followed by silence and the refrain:

O God of love we rejoice in you:
Reveal the glory of Christ in our lives.

(225) Prayer of Dedication

O God of steadfast love,
you have gathered us, your people, into praise,
cleansed us by your word of truth,
given us new hearts of flesh, not stone,
and called us to follow you in service:
Blessed be God, who daily bears us up
and who leads us into freedom and life

O God of suffering love,
you have shown us what it means to be obedient,
challenged us to a deeper commitment,
strengthened us to give more of ourselves,
and promised us that you will be with us always:
Blessed be God, who daily bears us up
and who leads us into freedom and life

O God of saving love,
you have made your home amongst us,
shared with us your vision and your dream,
encouraged us to pledge our lives to your purposes,
and enabled us to hope in your future for the world:
Blessed be God, who daily bears us up
and who leads us into freedom and life

(226) Prayer of Petition

Loving Jesus, Intercessor, as you have prayed for us to the Father:
Grant us a heart of love for all the world.

As you have given yourself to the uttermost
for the bereaved and the unprotected,
for the despairing and the desolate,
for prisoners, exiles and refugees,
for those who are oppressed, and for their oppressors,
for us, and for all humanity:
Grant us a heart of love for all the world.

Loving Jesus, Intercessor, as you pray for us now to the Father, release in us your devoted and healing grace, that we may be obedient to your truth, faithful to your hope, and witness to your glory:
Grant us a heart of love for all the world.

(227) Prayer of Dismissal

That the world may be judged by your humility and holiness:
Come, Lord Jesus, come!
That the people of God may live out your grace in sacrifice and compassion:
Come, Lord Jesus, come!
That the reign of God may be recognized throughout the world:
Come, Lord Jesus, come!

PENTECOST

Acts 2.1–21 (or Numbers 11.24–30); Psalm 104.24–34, 35b;
I Corinthians 12.3b–13 (or Acts 2.1–21); John 20.19–23
(or John 7.37–39)

GOD LOVES VARIETY

Presentation

Illustration: a display of various flowers. Discuss the variety of flowers. Which is the most beautiful? Is it possible to decide? Is it necessary to decide? Can we see the variety of flowering plants in our gardens as God's delight in diversity and difference? As evidence of the abundance and exuberance of God's creative Spirit? If it is easy to see this when considering flowers, why is it so hard when considering diversity amongst human beings, in ideas, preferences, opinions? If God loves diversity, and the Holy Spirit is constantly creating it, then how does Jesus want us to deal with the hurt that can be caused? Note that it is not the existence *of diversity which causes pain, but the way that we handle the differences between us.*

(228) Call to Worship

Psalm 104.33–34; John 7.37–38; *or* 19.19; Acts 2.1–4; I
Corinthians 12.3b–6; *or the following*

May the glory of God last for ever!
May God enjoy all that is made!
We will sing out to God as long as we live!
We will sing out to God while we have breath!
May our thoughts and hopes be pleasing to God!
For today and forever our God is our praise!

(229) Prayer of Invocation

Come, Holy Spirit, come:
as the wind out of the wild places where we do not wish to go;
as the breath of larger air which braces us and buffets us with all
that we would rather not face about ourselves, each other, and the
world.

Come, Holy Spirit, come:
as fire in the mind and joy in the heart;
making us see the saint in each other, and gathering us into a
hallowed unity where difference is valued, division reconciled, and
love does not accept less than perfect justice, a compelling
harmony.

Come, Holy Spirit, come:
– as speech which is heard and understood;
– as peace which does not mask the truth,
– as wonder which is not made small
    to match the littleness of our vision,
        but forged anew to strike a living spark in young and old;
– as love which will not hide.

(230) Prayer of Confession

Father forgive us,
that so often we have belittled the spiritual wealth of others.
We have despised their ecstasies, feared their enthusiasm,
carped at their experience, criticized their praise:
Father forgive us.

Father forgive us,
that so often we have belittled the spiritual wealth of others.
We have despised their liturgies, feared their intellectual questions,
carped at their traditions, criticized their praise:
Father forgive us.

Father forgive us, that so often we have resisted what we do not
understand, and have diminished what we do not share. In doing
so, we have missed the tongues of fire descending on your
disciples, and have refused, and grieved, your Spirit:
**Open our eyes and soften our hearts, that in generosity and love
we may listen to what your Spirit is teaching us
through other peoples' worship.
Open our eyes and soften our hearts,
that learning from each other,
we may find you taking us forward together
on the pilgrimage of joy.**

(231) Prayer of Thanksgiving

Generous Creator, you have poured out your grace on all people,
providing for our hunger, our need and our fear:
Generous God, we give you thanks and praise.

Compassionate Saviour, you have poured out your life for all people
so that mercy might heal our deepest wounds:
Compassionate Saviour, we give you thanks and praise.

Lavish Spirit, you have poured out your strength to refresh all people
in hope, in holiness and adoration:
Lavish Spirit, we give you thanks and praise.

Glorious God: Maker, Redeemer and Friend,
you have poured out your love on all people,
to hold the world in peace and to lead us into glory:
Glorious God, we give you thanks and praise.

(232) Prayer of Petition

Come, gentle Spirit, tend our wounds. Where we are afraid, breathe
on us courage and faithfulness, so that we may be loyal to each
other and honour our allegiance to Christ:
Come, gentle Spirit, tend our wounds.
Silence.

Where we distrust others, breathe on us faith and understanding, so
that we may be willing to explore their experience, even where it
challenges our own:
Come, gentle Spirit, tend our wounds.
Silence.

Where we are bruised, breathe on us repentance and peace, that we
may forgive others, as we have been forgiven, and find, through
reconciliation, that healing you have promised:
Come, gentle Spirit, tend our wounds.
Silence.

Where we are disheartened, breathe on us joy, so that we can
respect one another, honour one another, and go forward together
in truth and hope:
Come, gentle Spirit, tend our wounds.
Silence.

Come, gentle Spirit, tend our wounds:
**So that your spring of love may rise in our hearts and others
may bathe in your living waters.**

(233) Prayer of Dedication

For the times when we are amongst crowds and we must speak of
your love to people who are so different, from us and from each
other, in age and experience and need.
We call on your name, living God:
We rely on your power alone.

For the times when the emptiness echoes, and we must speak of
your love to one who is searching in fear and trust, not knowing
what the future may bring.
We call on your name, living God:
We rely on your power alone.

For the times when we are bewildered by so many names and
prayers and dreams, that we cannot see any pattern, any order, or
even decide which ones might be acceptable to you.
We call on your name, living God:
We rely on your power alone.

Loving Spirit, fresh breeze from the creative heart of God, work in
us that baptizing grace, so that through all the varieties of your gifts
we may see your wholeness;
through all the many ministries of your people, we may honour a
common allegiance to Christ;
and in all the different ways of serving others we may acknowledge
your inspiration:
**Bring us together, for the common good,
and to the glory of God, this day and forever.**

(234) Prayer of Dismissal

Live within the peace of God, that the love of Christ may nourish
you and the strength of the Spirit be your power and grace.

TRINITY SUNDAY

Genesis 1.1–2.4a; Psalm 8; II Corinthians 13.11–14;
Matthew 28.16–20

THREE AND ONE

Presentation
Illustration: Ice cubes, a jug of water and a steaming kettle.
Demonstrate how one element (water), can take three forms (solid,
liquid, gas). Though the Trinity remains a mystery, can examples of
'oneness and threeness' in the natural world help us glimpse the
possibility of someone being one and three in relationship with each
other, even one and three at the same time? Of course the
relationship between the three Persons of the Godhead is much more
complex than that between ice, water and steam. Rather, they are
bound together in a relationship of mutual and sacrificial love, co-
operation, understanding and service. This being so, what is the
place of human beings within this 'circle of blessing'?

(235) Call to Worship

Psalm 8.1a, 3–4, 9; Genesis 1.1–2; Matthew 28.16–20; *or*
II Corinthians 13.11–12; *or the following:*

All glory to our living God:
All praise to our Creator!
Glorious in splendour, glorious in majesty!
Let us worship God together!
All glory to our living God:
Let all the earth cry 'Glory!'

(236) Prayer of Adoration

One God, holy God, sovereign of creation, and source of all life
and blessing; you are all beauty, all justice, all truth.
In the beginning all that was made was good, and we could see
your image in ourselves, drawing all into harmony with your joy:
Glory to God! Sing praise!

One God, holy God, sovereign of creation, and source of all grace and hope, you are all compassion, all forgiveness, all mercy.
When we fell into wrongdoing you became our Saviour, and we could see how you carried our suffering on your cross, drawing all into healing through your resurrection:
Glory to God! Sing praise!

One God, holy God, sovereign of creation, and source of all energy and love, you are all variety, all plenty, all riches.
As we become partners in your purposes, we receive your word, and we can see order and diversity, pattern and fruitfulness drawing all into service, rest and praise:
Glory to God! Sing praise!

(237) Prayer of Confession

Forgive us, loving Creator, that we have failed to honour you with worship of simple purity and lives of humble truth.

Forgive us, loving Saviour, that we have failed to follow you in your path of devoted service and your offering of generous obedience.

Forgive us, loving Spirit, that we have failed to receive you in each other, in your care for all creation, and your witness to the Father and the Son.
Silence.

Accept us, Father-Mother God, through your own steadfast mercy, through the depth of your saving grace in your Son, and the cleansing of your Spirit who makes us whole; that we may give glory to your holy name, this day and forever.

(238) Prayer of Thanksgiving

For the grace of our Mother-Father God,
who hears our prayer, knows our need,
and offers us all things in love and trust:
Loving God, we give you thanks and praise.

For the compassionate understanding of our Saviour,
who died for our wrong, and lives for our right,
and offers us hope through generosity and faith:
Loving God, we give you thanks and praise.

For the community of the Spirit,
who is our Friend and our friendship, our Advocate and our
   strength,
and offers us a peace which cannot be explained or undermined:
Loving God, we give you thanks and praise.

(239) Prayer of Dedication

O God of the cross,
   with that same love which took our Lord Jesus Christ
   along the way of obedience and offering,
   encourage us to walk in his way.
O God of the Easter garden,
   with that same power which raised our Lord Jesus Christ
   from the dead,
   send us out to follow in his footsteps.
O God of the holy mountain,
   with that same strength which made disciples into apostles,
   equip us to teach and heal and serve in your name,
   from here to the ends of the earth,
   from now to eternity.

(240) Prayer of Dismissal

Matthew 28.16–20 *or* II Corinthians 13.11–14.

SUNDAY BETWEEN 29 MAY AND 4 JUNE INCLUSIVE

(if after Trinity Sunday. Ninth Sunday in Ordinary Time)

Genesis 6.9–22, 7.24, 8.14–19; and Psalm 46
or Deuteronomy 11.18–21, 26–28; and Psalm 31.1–5, 19–24;
Romans 1.16–17, 3.22b-28 (29–31); Matthew 7.21–29

FIRM FOUNDATIONS

Presentation
Illustration: build two 'houses' of children's bricks, one on 'rock' (a solid base such as a tea-tray) and the other on 'sand' (a base formed of overlapping pieces of paper). Demonstrate that a solid base is a better foundation than one liable to move or change. God's love and power are the firm foundation of our faith. Our faith, revealed through our obedience, is the firm foundation of our life of service and renewal.

(241) Call to Worship

Psalm 46.1–3, 10 *or* Psalm 31.1–2, 5 *or* Romans 1.16–17; *or the following:*

Father God, as the sun rises in the east,
you offer to us a brand new day.
As the sun dries the morning dew,
or melts the shining frost,
you give to us a fresh start.
Thank you for this day.
Thank you for this new beginning.
Help us now to live each moment to the full;
and as we worship you,
may we remember that your goodness and love
are the firm foundation of our life.

(242) Prayer of Adoration

For the strength that sustains the universe
through change and turmoil, death and birth:
We praise you.

For the generosity which reaches out to each one of us,
revealing how much you love us, and inviting us to love you in
return:
We praise you.

For the compassion that surrounds us with grace
and cares for us in each detail of our daily lives:
We praise you.

Loving God, for all your concern for us –
   stronger than the mountains,
   deeper than the oceans,
   more powerful than any storm,
   more gentle than the touch of a feather on our skin:
We praise you.

(243) Prayer of Acknowledgment

Father God, we place ourselves in your hands,
as those who believe in you.
So often we have pretended that nothing was wrong,
but we do realize what a mess we have made of our lives.
We have all fallen short of your glory,
and we want your help to put things right.
We believe that Jesus shows us the way to live,
and can help us to change.
By your Holy Spirit, make us more like Jesus,
building our lives on a solid base of obedience, trust and praise.

(244) Prayer of Thanksgiving

Thank you, Maker of all, that you never give up on us.
You are always making a new beginning,
you are always inviting us to start afresh with you.
Help us to step out again,
trusting, not in our own strength or goodness,
but in your love for us, and your power to strengthen us,
whatever may happen to us or to those we love.

(245) Prayer of Dedication

God is our shelter and strength,
always ready to help in times of trouble,
so we will not be afraid.
Even if we have lost what we most rely on,
our job, our friends, our home.
Whatever the future holds: **We will not be afraid.**

For God is our shelter and strength.
Even if we have lost our health,
experiencing pain and discomfort,
frustrated that we are no longer able to do
what we could do before.
Whatever the future holds: **We will not be afraid.**

For God is our shelter and strength.
Even if we have lost the one that we love,
someone we relied on,
someone who was there in good times and in bad.
Whatever the future holds: **We will not be afraid.**

For God is our shelter and strength.
But if we are afraid:
**Then remind us, Lord, of your loving presence,
and hold us tight as we cling to you.**

Prayers of Dismissal

(246)

Blessed be God,
who has shown us a wonderful love, a steadfast compassion.
Into God's hands we commit our spirits,
for the days to come, and for all time.

(247)

Read Psalm 46.10.

May the peace of God find you amidst the storms and troubles of
the world. May the peace of God keep you now and into all
eternity.

SUNDAY BETWEEN 5 AND 11 JUNE INCLUSIVE

(if after Trinity Sunday. Tenth Sunday in Ordinary Time)

Genesis 12.1–9 and Psalm 33.1–12 *or* Hosea 5.15–6.6
and Psalm 50.7–15; Romans 4.13–25; Matthew 9.9–13; 18–26

STEPPING OUT IN FAITH

Presentation
Illustration: footprints. Cut out a dozen large footprints in paper, lay them across the floor and encourage people to try walking in them. Draw out the difficulties of doing this if they are too far apart, or too close together; the dangers of slipping; the change in stride needed on different surfaces. As we 'follow in Christ's footsteps' he adapts his stride to match ours. Knowing this can give us the courage to let him lead us into the unknown, or into places where we would rather not go.

(248) Call to Worship

Psalm 33.1–5, Psalm 50.1–2, 14–15, *or* Hosea 6.1–3.

(249) Prayer of Adoration

Come, let us return to God, who is our husband and our friend.
O God, you are holy; you are all that is good and right and true;
you call us to live in your presence:
Loving God, we turn to you.
Silence.

Come, let us return to Christ, who is our redeemer and our friend.
O Christ, you are holy; you are all that is compassion and mercy;
you will heal our wounds:
Loving Jesus, we turn to you.
Silence.

Come, let us return to the Spirit, who is our companion and our
   friend.
O Spirit, you are holy; you are all that is gentleness and strength;
you will refresh our souls:
Loving Spirit, we turn to you.
Silence.

Loving God, receive us to yourself
in wisdom, grace and renewing fire,
that we may find ourselves accepted, purified, equipped
for service in your name, and to your praise and glory.

(250) Prayer of Confession

Lord, we make so many excuses when you call us to follow you:
'We're too young, we're too old, we're too busy, we're not strong
   enough.'
But you know what you're doing.
'Follow me,' you say, 'follow me, today, just as you are.'

But now is never the right time –
perhaps tomorrow, perhaps next week, perhaps next year.
But you know what you're doing.
'Follow me,' you say, 'follow me, today, just as you are.'

But it's too late for me –
there are others who could do it so much better.
It's time for me to take a back seat, give someone else a chance.
But you know what you're doing.
'Follow me,' you say, 'follow me, today, just as you are.'

But I'm not good enough,
I don't pray that often, and I find the Bible difficult to read.
Wouldn't it be better if you chose someone who's more spiritual?
But you know what you're doing.
'Follow me,' you say, 'follow me, today, just as you are.'

Help me, Lord, to hear your call;
to respond to it without delay, and with no more excuses,
trusting that you will provide all that is needed for the journey,
and that as I follow, so I will receive.

(251) Prayer of Acknowledgment

Father God, sometimes we try hard to get closer to you.
We try to do all the right things. We try to stop doing all the wrong
things. We even try to spend some time in prayer, to get you to
help us in this. And then, when you seem as far away as ever, we
find that you're there, right beside us. Closer than that, you're
actually at work within us.

You've always been there. You always will be there. The problem
is that we've been trying too hard: struggling to deserve your
attention, rather than gratefully accepting your love.

Thank you for Jesus, thank you for your Holy Spirit, thank you for
being who you are, our loving heavenly Father.

Silence.

Thank you, Lord.

(252) Prayer of Dedication

In faith, Abraham left familiar things:
May our faith welcome the opportunity of that which is new.
In faith, Abraham believed the impossible:
May our faith trust in your promises.
In faith, Abraham hoped, even when there was no reason for
hoping:
May our faith rely totally on you.
In faith, Abraham was filled with power:
May our faith strengthen us for service.
In faith, Abraham praised you:
May our faith lead us into worship, in the name of Christ.

(253) Prayer of Dismissal

Go with us, loving God, as we follow in the steps of Christ,
walking the narrow way.
Accompany us as one who shares the pleasures and perils of the
journey, and who breaks bread with us at each day's resting places.
Stay with us, as you have promised, from now until the close of the
age.

SUNDAY BETWEEN 12 AND 18 JUNE INCLUSIVE

(if after Trinity Sunday. Eleventh Sunday in Ordinary Time)

Genesis 18.1–15 (21.1–7) and Psalm 116.1–2, 12–19
or Exodus 19.2–8a and Psalm 100; Romans 5.1–8;
Matthew 9.35–10.8 (9–23)

CARRIED ON WINGS OF JOY

Presentation
Illustration: wings (birds, kites, gliders, planes etc.). Talk about the experience of flying, drawing out the way in which wings can carry considerable weight of passengers and cargo. Link this with the ability of smiles, fun, laughter and joy to 'carry' us and speed us on, even when the going is hard or even painful. Do we feel that God has a sense of humour? Do we notice the jokes in the stories and parables of Jesus? How do holiness and joy feed each other? As we celebrate God's good news together, how can 'wings of joy' speed our witness and caring?

(254) Call to Worship

Psalm 116.1–2 or 12–14, Psalm 100.1–2, *or* Romans 5.1–2.

(255) Prayer of Adoration

Can it be true, Lord?
That you, the creator and ruler of the whole universe, think of us as your very special friends, and that you want us to think of you in that way too?

Can it be true, Lord?
That you have chosen us to be your friends because you want to spend time with us, and join in what we are doing?

Can it be true, Lord?
That you will stick with us, even when other friends dump us? That you will stand up for us, even when others are nasty to us, and that you will never leave us?

Thank you, Lord, for your friendship.
Thank you for Jesus who has made this friendship possible for us.
Thank you for the Bible that helps our relationship to grow.
Thank you for your Holy Spirit who reminds us of your love for us.
We rejoice, that, because of Jesus, we now have you as our special
    friend.

Prayers of Acknowledgment

(256)

Listen, Lord, and help us to listen too.
Listen to the prayer in our hearts, and not just the words that spill
from our mouths.
Listen to the deep longings that we dare not speak about at all.
Listen to the anger and frustration that are hidden behind the polite
    mask.
Listen Lord, and help us to listen too.

(257)

We have wandered away, Lord,
lost sight of the Shepherd.
We are lost Lord, we don't know which way to turn.
Following each other, we are going around in circles.
Come and find us: take us home.
Silence.

And the Lord says, 'Here is my Shepherd.
He was never far away. Walk in trust, not in fear.
Love him enough to follow him, and he will bring you safe home.'

Prayers of Thanksgiving

(258)

Father God, thank you for smiles and laughter,
fun and humour, giggles and grins,
and friends with whom to share the joke.
Thank you that when things don't go quite according to plan, we
can still see the funny side of it.
Help us to keep on laughing, not at others, but at ourselves, as we
struggle to make sense of that which seems nonsense.
And in our laughter, give us relaxation and refreshment, so that we
can see familiar things in a new way.

(259)

For the love with which you meet us, so that we are received,
welcomed, heard:
We give you thanks and praise.
For the care with which you tend us, so that the deepest yearnings
of our secret hearts are known and understood:
We give you thanks and praise.
For the life with which you feed us, so that we are strengthened and
renewed:
We give you thanks and praise.
For the covenant into which you call us, to be your treasure, your
priests, your people:
We give you thanks and praise.
For the love into which you are drawing us, so that we are bound
with you in a communion of compassion and joy:
We give you thanks and praise.

(260) Prayer of Dismissal

Carry us on eagles' wings, living God,
that we may be supported by your light and joy
through pain and grief.

Carry us on eagles' wings, living God,
into places where your gentle touch of laughter
and your caress of grace,
can bring renewal, healing, hope.

SUNDAY BETWEEN 19 AND 25 JUNE INCLUSIVE

(if after Trinity Sunday. Twelfth Sunday in Ordinary Time)

Genesis 21.8–21 and Psalm 86.1–10, 16–17 *or* Jeremiah 20.7–13 and Psalm 69.7–10 (11–15) 16–18; Romans 6.1b–11; Matthew 10.24–39

SET FREE!

Presentation
Illustration: prisons. 'Imprison' a volunteer by covering him/her with a blanket and leaving them so during a reading or hymn. What did it feel like to be 'shut away' while everyone else was doing other things? How did it feel to be released? Discuss other situations where people have found a 'new lease of life' after release from illness, dependency, or through a change in circumstances. Link this with Paul's experience of having passed through death with Christ into a new life – a foretaste of the resurrection – in which he found freedom from fear and slavery to sin. How does God release us so that we can be at peace even in the midst of turmoil, pain, disease and death?

(261) Call to Worship

Psalm 86.8–10, or Psalm 69.16–18.

(262) Prayer of Adoration

O God our deliverer, you are our rest amidst work,
our stillness at the heart of struggle,
our calm in the face of difficulty.

Yours is the peace which comforts us when we grieve,
the force of creativity replacing destruction,
the hope which combats despair.

Release us, O God of deliverance,
into a new depth of your freedom,
where we may learn that independence which trusts in you alone,
and that resourcefulness which liberates the good in others.

As we are bound together in love of you,
and in service of our community,
may we encourage one another to claim our privileges as your
children, and free each other to praise.

Prayers of Acknowledgment and Petition

(263)

Loving Father, we need your help; because we are worried and
  afraid.
Loving Father, we need your advice; because we're in trouble and
  we don't know which way to turn.
Loving Father, we need your forgiveness; because we've done
  something of which now we are ashamed.
Loving Father, we need your presence; because our friends have
  left us and don't want to know.
Loving Father, we need Jesus, because only he can lead us out of
  this darkness.
Send your Son to us, we pray, and we will follow where he leads.
Send your Spirit to us, we pray, and we will have all that we need
  for the journey.

(264)

Lord, we want to live before we die:
and when those around us die,
we realize that life does not go on for ever.
Lord, we want to live before we die:
and when those around us are struck down by illness,
we realize that tomorrow may be very different from today.
Lord, we want to live before we die:
and when those around us are injured or maimed,
we realize that it could so easily have been us.
Lord, we want to live before we die:
thank you for each and every precious moment given to us.
Help us so to use each moment, that we discover your presence in
  it.
And as we live within that presence, so may you be alive in us,
living and reigning, in life as in death and as in the life to come.

(265)

Lord, we worry more about what others will think,
than about your reaction to what we do.
We try to please our friends more than we try to please you.
So often we take your love for granted.
Help us to understand the pain that you feel when we do what is
    wrong.
Help us to feel the sadness in your heart when we spoil ourselves
    and others.
And though your love will never end,
help us not to take it for granted.

(266) Prayer of Dedication

God of the narrow gate,
inspire in us the zeal which,
when criticized,
speaks a word of kindness;
when opposed, acts with gentle humility;
when persecuted, offers itself to the cross.
God of the narrow way,
inspire in us a praying that transforms our every moment
into loving fire, our every yearning into flame.

(267) Prayer of Dismissal

Let us walk in the world as strangers
who are yet at home within God's community,
empowered to live out his teaching,
free to love and praise.

SUNDAY BETWEEN 26 JUNE AND 2 JULY INCLUSIVE

(Thirteenth Sunday in Ordinary Time)

Genesis 22.1–14 and Psalm 13 *or* Jeremiah 28.5–9
and Psalm 89.1–4, 15–18; Romans 6.12–23; Matthew 10.40–42

FREE GIFT

Presentation

*Illustration: a product advertising a 'free gift.' Talk about our
experience of free gifts: are they worth anything, or is it true that
'there is no such thing as a free lunch'. Draw out the spiritual truth
that 'our gift is someone else's sacrifice'; that love and creativity are
free but not cheap; that grace also involves discipline; that the
process of forgiveness includes judgment, repentance and repara-
tion. In what ways has God sacrificed so that we might receive? In
what ways do we need to sacrifice so that others may receive? And
if we know this, how can we receive such generosity – from God and
from others – with humility rather than guilt?*

(268) Call to Worship

Psalm 13.5–6 *or* Psalm 89.1–2, and 5 (or Psalm 89.15–18); *or the
following:*

Welcome, Lord Jesus, to this time of worship.
We gather here in your name,
to offer our thanks and praise,
and we are glad that you are here with us.

Through you we welcome the one who sent you:
we welcome God himself;
and we pray that in this time of praise
we will know that your Spirit is moving among us.

We welcome you, Lord Jesus:
now guide us in our adoration
so that all that is said and done may bring honour to your name.

(269) Prayer of Adoration, Acknowledgment and Thanksgiving

Living God, in sunshine and rain you provide.
In times of plenty and in times of famine, you provide.
When things seem hopeful, or when hope is draining away, you
    provide.
You are the source of all goodness:
you cradle the present and future carefully in your hands.
You are all that is needed for whatever the future may hold.
And you will give us all that we require.
Silence.

Loving Jesus, in summer and in winter you care for us.
In times of joy and in times of sorrow you care for us.
When peace is present and when peace is swallowed up in conflict
    and hatred, you care for us.
You show us the meaning of compassion:
you stretch out your arms for us upon the cross.
Your mercy embraces all, your grace is sufficient for our every
    need.
Silence.

Holy Spirit, in health and in sickness you inspire us.
In times of strength and in times of weakness you inspire us.
When life is vigorous, and when life is diminished or destroyed,
    you inspire us.
You are the truth of our loving:
you offer yourself as help and guide, support and comfort.
Your power wells up in our hearts and in the midst of our
    community,
pointing to the gifts you have given us.
Silence.

We acknowledge our need, we thank you for your care:
Guard us in our sorrows, deepen us in faith.
Help us to face each day, renew us in your grace.

(270) Prayer of Petition

Lord God, sometimes you seem so far away:
are you hiding yourself from me, or am I hiding from you?
Sometimes, I wonder why I bother to pray at all:
my words sound so empty,
ringing hollow as they echo around the room.
Are you there? Are you listening? Do you care?
Look at me, O Lord, and answer me,
lift me up and give me hope.
I rely upon you: you are all I have.
In the past I have known your strength and comfort:
help me now!
Open my eyes to see your goodness and your love.

(271) Prayer of Dismissal

Follow God into the places of pain, taking the generosity of grace.
Follow God into the places of service, taking the gentleness of
love.
Follow God into the places of thanksgiving, taking songs of joy.

SUNDAY BETWEEN 3 AND 9 JULY INCLUSIVE

(Fourteenth Sunday in Ordinary Time)

Genesis 24.34–38, 42–49, 58–67 and Psalm 45.10–17
(*or* Canticle: Song of Solomon 2.8–13); *or* Zechariah 9.9–12 and
Psalm 145.8–14; Romans 7.15–25a; Matthew 11.16–19, 25–30

BOUND TOGETHER IN LOVE

Presentation

Illustration: a wedding ring. List the reasons why people get married, and what they look to gain from marriage. Draw out the fact that these reasons can include both high ideals (love of the partner) and practical needs (financial security). Then list the factors which help people to grow in marriage. Reflect together: can we liken our relationship with God to a marriage? If so, what does this say about our reasons for responding to God in the first place, and what does it suggest about the qualities we must develop in order to allow our covenant-bond to develop and deepen? What qualities become most important when we remember that our relationship with God – like our other relationships – is rarely perfect.

(272) Call to Worship

Psalm 45.1–3 *or* Psalm 145.1–3, *or the following:*

The Lord is here – in faith and in praise:
God binds us together in love.
The Lord is here – in joy and in hope:
God binds us together in love.
The Lord is here – for now and forever:
God binds us together in love.

(273) Prayer of Adoration and Thanksgiving

God our provider and life-giver, source of love and hope,
maker of relationships, giver of beauty and gentleness,
revealer of hidden things –
in you we live and move and exist.
You are our true home:
We praise you, O Lord. We thank you.

That you have reached out to us through the love of Jesus,
touching our hearts and minds, making us your people.
That we can come from different places,
with different hopes and needs,
and find that we are one in you.
That we can come in joy and in sadness,
and find you holding us in love:
We praise you, O Lord. We thank you.

That you have given us your church,
and drawn us together as your people.
That you help us create space
so that we can be aware of your presence.
That you place us within a community
in which we are valued and loved.
That you love us all in our variety,
and that you love us to the uttermost:
We praise you, O Lord. We thank you.

(274) Prayer of Confession

Hear us, O God, as we ask forgiveness:
for the hurt we have caused you,
and the hurt we have caused those around us:
Lord, please forgive us.
For the unkind words we have used,
and the things we have failed to do:
Lord, please forgive us.
For our unwillingness to forgive,
while depending on your forgiveness of us:
Lord, please forgive us.
For our selfishness and greed,
for our jealousy and pride:
Lord, please forgive us.
For the prejudices we carry,
and the way we accept the unacceptable:
Lord, please forgive us.
For the sins of our family,
for the sins of our community:
Lord, please forgive us.

For the damage to our environment,
for the damage to our nation and our world:
Lord, please forgive us.
Compassionate God, hold us when we stumble,
pick us up when we fall:
We ask it through Jesus Christ our Lord.

*The Call to Worship could be repeated as an affirmation and
thanksgiving*

(275) Prayer of Dedication

Lord, what we have, we offer,
our time, our commitment, our money.
But most of all we offer ourselves.
Help us to be used in your work,
to encourage each other in giving and serving,
and to extend your given kingdom of love.

(276) Prayer of Dismissal

Lord, as we go, nourish our vision,
build our confidence, and enfold us in your care:
You have bound us together in love.

SUNDAY BETWEEN 10 AND 16 JULY INCLUSIVE

(Fifteenth Sunday in Ordinary Time)

Genesis 25.19–34 and Psalm 119.105–112 *or* Isaiah 55.10–13 and Psalm 65. (1–8) 9–13; Romans 8.1–11; Matthew 13.1–9, 18–23

THE SOWER

Presentation

Illustration: sowing 'seed'. Compile a list of gifts, blessings or 'reasons to be thankful' and write each one on a paper 'seed'. Distribute these amongst the congregation. Draw out the fact that the seed has fallen into a variety of environments. How do those who have received a seed feel about the one which has fallen to them? Can they use it? Is it relevant? Can it challenge them to look again at their priorities or consider a new area of growth? Does it highlight an area of pain? If so, how do we respond, bearing in mind God's desire for us to experience new life, and life to the full? What are the feelings and failings which cause us to reject God's gifts?

(277) Call to Worship

Psalm 119.105, 111 *or* Psalm 65.1–4, *or the following:*
God is the source of our life:
He journeys with us in love.
God is the giver of good:
He journeys with us in love.
God is the sower of grace:
He journeys with us in love.
God is our strength and our hope:
He journeys with us in love.

(278) Prayer of Adoration and Thanksgiving

Lord of life, you have sown the seeds of your life throughout creation.
You have filled the earth with beauty and wonder:
We praise you.

You have found us and made us your own:
We praise you.
You have made us aware of our worth:
We praise you.
You have put songs of praise in our hearts:
We praise you.
You have placed us in community and called us to love:
We praise you.
You have given us art and music, imagination and memory:
We praise you.
You have given us work and technology, invention and skill:
We praise you.
You have given us unlimited resources in your Spirit, and the grace
    to give each other hope:
We praise you.
You have given us Jesus, and all things in him.
We praise you.

(279) Prayer of Confession

God, our provider and pain-bearer, we make confession:
For not understanding the good news, distorting it to suit ourselves:
We ask forgiveness.
For deceiving and manipulating others, and using clever words to
    mask our true motives:
We ask forgiveness.
For our contempt of serious things, taking the easy option for the
    sake of convenience:
We ask forgiveness.
For greed and ambition, so that we get as much as we can while
    others have nothing:
We ask forgiveness.
For encouraging favouritism, and for carrying bitterness in our
    hearts:
We ask forgiveness.
For giving up too easily in the face of discipline or difficulty;
renouncing what is precious, for the sake of passing pleasures:
We ask forgiveness.
For our destructive influence on people and situations:
We ask forgiveness.
Silence.

Generous God, we offer to you the thin soil of our lives, the hard roads and rocky places where little can grow and life has been scorched and withered. We offer, too, the weeds and the thorns to your thorough, pruning hand. Deal gently with us, generous God, for your mercy's sake. Inspire us with visions of your glory, refresh our spirits by your grace and hold us in your love, now and always.

(280) Prayer of Dedication

God, our strength and our hope, you have given to us more than we can say. As we offer you these gifts we dedicate to you our work, our dreams and our lives. May we open our eyes, our ears and our hearts to your presence. Touch our lives and help us to grow in the kingdom you have established in our hearts and in the world.

(281) Prayer of Dismissal

May we go from this place grateful for all that you have given us.
May we go into our daily round encouraged by all that you have sown in our lives.
May we go into your world to set others free to receive your love, your grace and your offering, this day and forever.

SUNDAY BETWEEN 17 AND 23 JULY INCLUSIVE

(Sixteenth Sunday in Ordinary Time)

Genesis 28.10–19a and Psalm 139.1–12, 23–24 (*or* Wisdom of Solomon 12.13, 16–19) *or* Isaiah 44.6–8 and Psalm 86.11–17; Romans 8.12–25; Matthew 13.24–30, 36–43

WEEDS

Presentation

Illustration: weeds. If possible, display a patch of soil in which weeds and flowers are growing together. Talk about the difficulty of weeding overgrown flower beds and sorting out the weeds from the desired plants. Draw out the temptation to just scythe it all back and dig it all up (or spray with weedkiller!). Why does God deal so differently with us? Does this help us to understand why some forms of suffering might be allowed to remain in the world? Is it our experience that all things work together for good, and that God can be found both in the light and in the dark? How does the vision of God's love, care and glory help to turn the place of stones into a gate of heaven?

(282) Call to Worship

Psalm 139.1–4 *or* Psalm 86.1–4 (or 11–12) *or* Isaiah 44.6–8a, *or the following:*

This is the day that God has made holy:
Let us rejoice and be glad!
This is the day that God calls us together:
Let us rejoice and be glad!
This is the day that God calls us to praise:
Let us rejoice and be glad!

(283) Prayer of Adoration and Thanksgiving

O God of the universe, we thank you for your daily care:
you know us completely, you know all our needs,
you are familiar with all our ways.
We give thanks to you with all our hearts:
We will glorify your name forever.

We thank you for the natural world,
for its wonder and variety,
for the beauties of form and colour and texture
in which we can delight.
We give thanks to you with all our hearts:
We will glorify your name forever.

We praise you for the gift of loving and being loved,
for friendships and understanding.
We give thanks to you with all our hearts:
We will glorify your name forever.

We thank you for language, history and culture,
for learning and imagination which open up the world to us;
for visions and dreams which challenge and inspire us.
We give thanks to you with all our hearts:
We will glorify your name forever.

When uncertainty clouds our joy, and we despair of humanity,
you encourage and reassure us through the stories of old,
and the example of Jesus,
who fashions our faith through his death and resurrection,
We give thanks to you with all our hearts:
We will glorify your name forever.

Help us to hear you during this time of worship,
through the songs we sing, through the words we hear,
through the conversation we share:
**Guide us in the way of hope,
that the place of stones may become the gate of heaven
and we may live to your praise and glory.**

(284) Prayer of Confession

Lord, we have failed you in words, thoughts and actions.
We have not lived as your children,
but as people who have no inheritance or hope.
Forgive us for the words we have spoken to wound and hurt.
Forgive us for thoughts which we have encouraged
and which have led to guilt and pain.
Forgive us for the actions we have taken hastily
and which cast a shadow on our lives.
Forgive us for the way our wrongdoing is entangled
with the wrongdoing of others:
**Lord of mercy, with that generosity which you show towards all
creation, forgive what we have been,
help us to turn aside from despair and decay,
and make us the people we ought to be,
your children of grace and love.**

(285) Meditation

to follow the reading of the Gospel.

Voice 1:   Lord, why is it that whatever I do can be spoilt by
              someone else? I created a beautiful garden and someone
              has ruined it by sowing weeds. How can I get rid of
              them? How long do I wait for them to die?
              Silence.

Voice 2:   Lord, my life is beautiful and colourful: you made me
              this way. But I know that something isn't quite as it
              should be. What is wrong, Lord? How do I find out?
              And how do I uproot those things which are not as you
              want them to be?
              Silence.

Voice 3:   Lord, I'm puzzled: how did you deal with weeds? You
              must have done something. They are not there when I
              catch a glimpse of you in others.
              Silence.

(286) Meditation

The place of stones becomes an open stair,
a gate, a long ascending path from earth to heaven.
And I, who came alone, downhearted,
to a barren country; caught by night
amongst the consequences of my failings,
my deliberate sins – no, I had not looked for grace.

But grace it was, and is,
to find here in the wilderness,
the companionship of angels, and the pledge of Presence,
guiding, gifting and enfolding future days.

(287) Prayer of Dedication

O God of the universe, you are the first and the last, the beginning
and the end. All that we have comes from you.
All we have and all we are, we offer to you, living God.
May what we have offered be used to make a difference to the
needs around us, to set people free from pain so that they can live
in hope. We ask it in faith, through Jesus Christ our Lord.

Prayers of Dismissal

(288)

May the God of love hold you when you travel alone,
may the God of peace surround you in the barren place of stones,
may the God of hope inspire you with a dream of kingdom come,
now and always.

(289)

May the God of all generosity
guard you in your discipleship and keep you in grace,
this day and forever.

SUNDAY BETWEEN 24 AND 30 JULY INCLUSIVE

(Seventeenth Sunday in Ordinary Time)

Genesis 29.15–28 and Psalm 105.1–11, 45b (*or* Psalm 128)
or I Kings 3.5–12 and Psalm 119.129–136; Romans 8.26–39;
Matthew 13.31–33, 44–52

THE PEARL OF GREAT PRICE

Presentation

Illustration: pearls. Simulate a pearl with a white ball and an oyster made with two almost-circles of card joined in one place forming a hinge. Illustrate how a pearl is formed: any grit entering the oyster is an irritant – the creature protects itself by coating the piece of grit with a hard layer of mother-of-pearl. Before human beings learned how to stimulate this process artificially, pearls were rare, and, consequently, highly desirable and expensive. What are the modern equivalents for which we might be prepared to give up everything? If no material object is that desirable, what about other things, such as a loving partner, or a child, or health, or the fulfilment of a dream? How do we decide which desires are worth waiting for, working for, sacrificing for – and which not?

(290) Call to Worship

Psalm 105.1–3 *or* 1–5 *or* Psalm 119.132–3, 135, *or the following:*

Turn towards us, Lord of grace,
for you are always loving towards those who turn to you:
Steady our steps as we seek you,
for you are faithful to all your promises.
We shall praise you and not be afraid.

(291) Prayer of Adoration and Thanksgiving

Maker of worlds out of love; giver of life;
source of patience; bringer of order out of chaos;
God of all people:
We praise and adore you.

When we were lost, you were looking for us.
When we came to our senses we saw that you had been there all
the time, calling to us in our absence and our want.
God of all people:
We praise and adore you.

When we were lonely, you were waiting for us.
When we became humble we saw that you had been there all the
time, reaching through our isolation and despair.
God of all people:
We praise and adore you.

When we were battered and hurt, you saw and understood.
When we became vulnerable we saw that you had been there all the
time, offering healing in the hands that touched our wounds.
God of all people:
We praise and adore you.

God of small and unpromising beginnings,
of the undeserving, the lazy and the indifferent,
of those who are hungry and poor and fragile,
the exile, the exhausted and the refugee,
we praise you that you reveal yourself in surprising places:
that you are always there for us,
helping us to laugh, to love and to find hope;
that you give plenty where nothing was expected,
an abundance where the cup was full.
God of all people:
We praise and adore you.

(292) Prayer of Confession

Merciful God, as we come together in our need
we offer to you our sins and the sins of the world.
For our lack of compassion to those in want:
We ask forgiveness.
For the way we have marred your image in us and in others:
We ask forgiveness.
For our vindictive and selfish ways:
We ask forgiveness.
For seeking power for our own selfish desires, rather than service
    of the kingdom:
We ask forgiveness.

For resisting changes that would bring new life:
We ask forgiveness.
For being a stumbling block to the kingdom:
We ask forgiveness.
For the inadequate way in which we love:
We ask forgiveness.

(293) Prayer of Petition

Merciful God, touch us with your forgiving power,
that we may wait with patience for your day of blessing,
and work with zeal for the good you will for all.
Glorious God, touch us with your generous love:
that we may work in faith for justice,
and wait in peace for the revealing of your rule and reign.

(294) Prayer of Dedication

God, you gave Jesus to us
as a treasure found where we least expected it,
as the one prize worth everything we have.
With a generosity beyond our dreams, he offered his life, freely, to
us and to all the world.
What we offer now are symbols of our love for you, and a token of
your great investment in us.
Honour our faith, that from these small beginnings may grow
evidence of your love, justice and peace.

(295) Prayer of Dismissal

As we go into the world,
may God's love be at work in us in unexpected ways;
may the wisdom of Jesus enlighten us with surprises;
and may the Holy Spirit intercede for us in our silences of
bewilderment and pain, now and always.

SUNDAY BETWEEN 31 JULY AND 6 AUGUST INCLUSIVE

(Eighteenth Sunday in Ordinary Time)

Genesis 32.22–31 and Psalm 17.1–7, 15 *or* Isaiah 55.1–5
and Psalm 145.8–9, 14–21; Romans 9.1–5; Matthew 14.13–21

FEEDING THE MULTITUDE

Presentation
Illustration: five loaves and two fish. List the 'big problems' of the world which we find daunting by their huge size and bewildering complexity. Then list the resources which are available to help us wrestle with them. Discuss how the two lists relate together. Do the resources available match the scope of the task? How do we feel about any disparities? What does God expect us to do with the resources he makes available to us for his purposes? How does he expect us to respond to problems which are too big for us to handle, or forces which threaten to overwhelm us? What blessings come from wrestling with these big issues?

(296) Call to Worship

Psalm 17.6–7 *or* Psalm 55.1–3, *or the following:*

God holds us in love:
We sing out our praise.
God holds us in peace:
We sing out our praise.
God holds us in joy:
We sing out our praise.

(297) Prayer of Adoration and Thanksgiving

Living God, author of life, sustainer of hope, teacher of truths,
giver of love to a broken world, we praise and adore you.
Throughout the ages you have journeyed with your people,
revealing yourself through stories and mystery.
You have provided for their needs in desolate places.
You have guided them by day and night: blessing them when they
wrestled with you; forgiving them when they rejected you.

Through your persistence with them, we can see your love and
truth at work to change their lives – and ours.
As we worship, we celebrate your love for us,
and our love for each other.
We praise you because you hear the cries of your people.
We praise you because you gave your Son on the cross.
We praise you because you bring good out of evil.
We give thanks that despite our disobedience and selfishness, we
can know the transforming power of your mercy and compassion.
God our Father, worker of miracles – work in our hearts today so
Jesus can become our Saviour and our hope.

(298) Prayer of Confession

Loving God, when we are tested by your truth and our frailty, grant
    us:
– courage to offer ourselves as we are
– honesty to ask for mercy and healing.

For our neglect of family and friends: **Father, forgive us.**
For depending only on ourselves: **Father, forgive us.**
For our inadequate response to those in need: **Father, forgive us.**
For rejecting your love in others: **Father, forgive us.**
For failing to encourage the sad and despairing: **Father, forgive us.**
For our lack of vision: **Father, forgive us.**
For our poor discipleship: **Father, forgive us.**
For indifference towards our responsibilities: **Father forgive us.**

Loving God, as you move within us to change us, take from us all
that is negative and destructive, and replace it with freedom and
justice, generosity and peace, through Jesus Christ our Lord.

(299) Prayer of Petition

God of compassion, may we never rest satisfied with a religion
from which any of your people are excluded. May we never live
easily in a community from which any are shut out. May your love
lead us on in faith, and hope, and generosity, until all are invited,
welcomed, fed and healed.

(300) Prayer of Dedication

Lord, you provide all that we need.
Increase our faith so that we may offer even the little we have,
trusting in your faithfulness, power and grace,
for ourselves, and for the needs of the world.

(301) Prayer of Dismissal

Gracious Lord,
as we have wrestled with your mystery,
so dismiss us with your blessing.
As we have brought to you our offering,
so send us out renewed:
**Strengthen us in faith, uphold us in love,
and rekindle the hope in our hearts.**

SUNDAY BETWEEN 7 AND 13 AUGUST INCLUSIVE

(Nineteenth Sunday in Ordinary Time)

Genesis 37.1–4, 12–28 and Psalm 105.1–6, 16–22, 45b *or*
I Kings 19.9–18 and Psalm 85.8–13; Romans 10.5–15;
Matthew 14.22–33

CALLING ON GOD IN NEED

Presentation

Illustration: a telephone. How do we go about making an emergency call? What agencies are there to help in time of need? What do they need to know about us? What kinds of help can they offer? Do we find it easy to receive their help? When family, friends or neighbours try to help – perhaps in less dramatic circumstances – what factors might 'get in the way' to make their intervention unwelcome or inappropriate? Does the discussion throw any light on how we appeal to God, what God knows about us, and how it can sometimes be difficult to ask for, and receive, God's response? How can we be more open to God speaking in unexpected ways? Can we as 'helpers' be more sympathetic to the sensitivities of those we are trying to serve?

(302) Call to Worship

Psalm 105.1–3 *or* Psalm 85.8–9.

(303) Prayer of Adoration

God of the universe, Lord of eternity,
you speak in signs and visions,
whispers in the silence, the promptings of conscience,
the joy of the heart: **We praise you.**

God of all people, Lord of humanity,
you approach us in the dramas of history,
the detail of our every day hopes for our families and friends,
the peace of communion: **We praise you.**

God of all ages, Lord of the church,
you renew us through the resurrection of Jesus,
the Spirit's life outpoured, dreams of justice and freedom,
and the power of prayer: **We praise you.**

(304) Prayer of Confession

to follow the reading from Genesis

O God, it is not always easy to live in a family. Like Joseph we
sometimes tell tales about sisters or brothers and then no one is
happy:
Lord, forgive our selfish ways and help us to love.

O God, it is hard being a parent, trying to be fair and just, and, like
Jacob, often getting it wrong:
Lord, forgive our failings and help us to love.

O God, one wrong so often leads to another, then we find it hard to
avoid hurting others and ourselves:
Lord, forgive our weaknesses and help us to love.

(305) Prayer of Petition

Help, I am afraid: who can I turn to?
– on the doormat there is the final demand and the overdrawn bank
  statement.
– my homework is unfinished and I have that test at school today.
– here comes that playground bully and there is nowhere to hide.
– today we have the meeting when the redundancies will be
  announced.
Help, I am afraid: who can I turn to?

Lord Jesus,
help us to see you when we are afraid.
Help us to hear your voice calling us when our faith is weak.
Help us to feel the strength of your arms supporting and lifting us
when we are sinking.
Lord Jesus, give us your peace.

(306) Prayer of Dedication

God of compassion, Lord of all grace,
you call us to give ourselves without holding back,
to leave all that might hinder us,
and cast aside all that is evil:
Build us in faith, hope and love,
that as we see you, so we may follow you,
and as you live, so may we live,
in joy and praise.

(307) Prayer of Dismissal

O God who calls us to follow in the way of Jesus:
let us go out with joy into your world,
let us share your love with those we meet,
let us serve the peoples with humility,
let us live with your blessing.

SUNDAY BETWEEN 14 AND 20 AUGUST INCLUSIVE

(Twentieth Sunday in Ordinary Time)

Genesis 45.1–15 and Psalm 133 *or* Isaiah 56.1, 6–8
and Psalm 67; Romans 11.1–2a, 29–32; Matthew 15. (10–20) 21–28

WORKING TOWARDS UNITY

Presentation
Illustration: bridges. Display and discuss pictures or models of bridges. What are the different parts of a bridge? (foundations, a span carrying a road or railway, some means of support). Draw out the fact that each of these parts needs the other. Link these with the task of bridge-building in human relationships. What are the foundations on which we must build? With what attitudes, activities or qualities do we build a 'span' strong enough to carry us – and others – into pilgrimage and reconciliation? And from where do we derive our support?

(308) Call to Worship

Psalm 133.1, 3b *or* Psalm 67.1–3.

(309) Prayer of Adoration

O God of all people, we come to worship you because you make us one great rainbow family, with different gifts and abilities, ages and experiences, backgrounds and insights.
May the peoples praise you, O God:
May all the peoples praise you.

O God of all people, we come to rejoice in your loving power which overcomes the barriers we build between ourselves.
May the peoples praise you, O God:
May all the peoples praise you.

O God of all people, we come to celebrate together, to receive your forgiveness of our sins, to hear your good news and to go in your name to proclaim your love.
May the peoples praise you, O God:
May all the peoples praise you.

(310) Prayer of Confession

God of truth and mercy, we make our confession:
We have not always maintained justice in our midst.
We have not always done what is right.
We have not always looked for your saving help.

We have often despised those who are different.
We have refused a welcome to the stranger in our midst.
We have mocked the devotions of others,
and criticized their offerings and their prayers.

May we imitate the compassion and justice of Jesus,
holding to the truth and offering ourselves to your transforming
   grace.
May we learn to see him in the humanity and faith of others,
hearing the Spirit in their prayers, and working with them
to create a community where all belong.

(311) Prayer of Dedication

using three voices

Voice 1:   He is strange . . .
Voice 2:   She is weird . . .
Voice 3:   They are different . . .
Voice 1:   We are special . . .
Voice 2:   I don't get on with that sort . . .
Voice 3:   I don't feel at ease with them . . .
Voice 1:   I don't trust them . . .
Voice 2:   O Lord, you call us to welcome you in the stranger, in the outcast, in the refugee.
Voice 3:   O Lord, you call us to have compassion on the disadvantaged, the homeless, the poor.
Voice 1:   O Lord, you challenge us to be hospitable, to discover you in those who are different from us. You continually invite us to bridge the gaps, to open the doors, to break down the walls which we create to make us separate.
Voice 2:   O Lord, help us and be with us as we seek . . .
Voice 3:   . . . to cross the chasms of misunderstanding and fear
Voice 1:   . . . to dare open our doors which shut out and exclude
Voice 2:   . . . to dismantle the walls which divide and separate.
Voice 3:   So that we may live together, share together, learn together, celebrate together and together be one people.

(312) Prayer of Dismissal

God be merciful and bless us.
Look on us with kindness, so that the whole world may know your will, so that all nations may know your saving help.
May the peoples praise you, O God:
May all the peoples praise you.

SUNDAY BETWEEN 21 AND 27 AUGUST INCLUSIVE

(Twenty-first Sunday in Ordinary Time)

Exodus 1.8–2.10 and Psalm 124 *or* Isaiah 51.1–6 and Psalm 138;
Romans 12.1–8; Matthew 16.13–20

THOSE WHO DARE

Presentation

*Illustration: 'Go on, I dare you!' Describe or enact a childhood
'dare'. What kinds of mischief do we get up to because we are dared
to do things by others? Where does the courage – or foolhardiness –
come from to do such things? Is there a more positive meaning to
'daring'? Do we agree that those who dare can achieve great
things? What of the need to show daring or defiance in the face of
injustice or evil, or overwhelming odds? If it is true that 'daring' is
a double-edged attitude, how do we decide between that daring
which is appropriate for a Christian, and that which is not?*

(313) Call to Worship

Psalm 138.4–6, *or* Isaiah 51.1, 4; *or the following:*

Glory to God, who is our strength and our help!
Glory to God! Glory to God!
Glory to God, who has saved us from evil!
Glory to God! Glory to God!
Glory to God, who is our strength and deliverer!
Glory to God! Glory to God!
Glory to God who is wisdom and love!
Glory to God! Glory to God!

(314) Prayer of Adoration and Acknowledgment

a prayer for two voices and congregation

Voice 1: Hear this, if you want to do what is right. Hear this, if
you want to seek the Lord.

Voice 2: God has given us the stories of the past for our
inspiration; and in the present, the power of the Spirit to
renew our souls.

Silence.

We praise you, Lord:
We will find joy and gladness in your presence.
We will give thanks and sing songs of praise.

Voice 1: Hear this, the teaching of God goes out to all nations.
Hear this, the justice of God is a light to all peoples.

Voice 2: God has set us free from evil forever. The rule and reign
of the Lord will never come to an end.

Silence.

We praise you, Lord:
We will find joy and gladness in your presence.
We will give thanks and sing songs of praise.

Voice 1: Hear this, if you want to know what is right and holy.
Hear this, if you want God's teaching to live in your
hearts.

Voice 2: God says, do not be afraid of the forces arrayed against
you. Do not be dismayed at the overwhelming power of
wrong.

Silence.

We praise you, Lord:
We will find joy and gladness in your presence.
We will give thanks and sing songs of praise.

(315) Prayer of Thanksgiving

O God of the wilderness, you bring forth life from the dry deserts
of our lives. We rejoice in the beauty of colours, fragrances and
textures amid the greyness and dullness of much of our living. May
we see and celebrate signs of new growth in each other:
Let us live in trust.

O God of the refugee and the exile, you offer hope and peace when
we feel far from home. We offer our praise for the discovery that
you are present in the unfamiliar and the unknown. May we find
your peace where we are:
Let us live in joy.

O God of the forgotten peoples, you bring love, acceptance and
worth to all who turn to you. We give thanks for your saving touch
which gives us value, purpose and hope. May we stand tall and put
our confidence in your ways of recreation:
Let us live anew.

(316) Meditation

Daring God, you call us to be different, to stand out from the crowd. It is much safer to be the same as everyone else, to blend in, to be hidden, a sort of undercover agent for you.

But then, if we do live as you would like, we are bound to stand out, for you say that we should not think just about ourselves, but should work together for you.

You have put us in a team where everyone has a part. We are all good at different things. If we all pitch in together it really does work. We have to trust each other, and encourage each other, and doing things in that way makes us stand out from the crowd. I don't mind so much if there are others who are different with me.

(317) Prayer of Dedication

You tell us to go, when we would rather stay.
You tell us to share when we would rather keep what we have.
You tell us to grow when we would rather be still.
You tell us to risk when we would rather be safe.
O Lord find the weak chinks in our armour and open us to the ways of your loving Spirit, who moulds and reshapes us into the people you would have us be – willing and open, humble, and true to your way of love in your world.

(318) Prayer of Dismissal

Creator God, enable us to offer your blessing in our loving, and your peace in our serving.

Jesus, Son of the living God, lead us into the demands of our lives with hope, so that we meet with you in our homes, our work, our places of learning.

Emboldening Spirit, show us how you are active in those with whom we live and work and play.

SUNDAY BETWEEN 28 AUGUST AND 3 SEPTEMBER INCLUSIVE

(Twenty-second Sunday in Ordinary Time)

Exodus 3.1–15 and Psalm 105.1–6, 23–26, 45c *or* Jeremiah 15.15–21 and Psalm 26.1–8; Romans 12.9–21; Matthew 16.21–28

INVESTING IN LIFE!

Presentation

Illustration: a building society passbook or card. When we make a financial investment, we take the risk of a set-back, but we expect to receive a much larger return in the long run. We are not only investing our money, but also our trust in that vision of a larger future. Consider how God asks us to take a similar risk, and make a similar investment. The bad news is that our risk includes a cross. We may find ourselves wounded by loving, our resources drained. The good news is that our return is life, here and hereafter.

(319) Call to Worship

Psalm 105.1–3 or 1–4 *or* Jeremiah 15.1b; *or the following:*

We sing a hymn of thanksgiving,
and tell of your wonderful deeds:
We love the place where you live, O Lord,
the place where your glory dwells.

(320) Prayer of Adoration and Acknowledgment

to follow either Old Testament or Epistle.

God of life, we praise you:
renew in us your fire of grace,
that we may burn with the love
that transforms and heals,
but does not consume.
God of life, we praise you:
renew in us your spring of truth,
that we may be your messengers of peace,
channels of holy well-being in our communities.

God of life, we praise you:
we offer to you our rigid tongues,
our frozen hearts, our empty hands,
asking that your love and mercy, hope and joy,
may warm us, fill us, free us, sing in us,
and lead the world to praise.

(321) Prayer of Thanksgiving

Let us pray:
Praise to you, O God – for you are a God who does not hide from
the suffering and hardships in this world.
Praise to you, O God – for you are in touch with those who are
afraid and are hungry.
Praise to you, O God – for you work in hidden and mysterious
ways to bring life out of death, hope from despair, and
forgiveness for our sins.
Praise to you, O God – for being here in our worship, for being in
the difficulties we face, for offering us chances to be made
whole.
Praise to you, O God.

(322) Prayer of Petition

We like to protect ourselves from pain and discomfort,
we like to avoid conflict,
we like to have enemies that are far away and out of sight.
Jesus, you call us to be alongside those who hurt,
to offer your gentleness;
to be near enough to our enemies to touch them,
and to know their needs for prayer;
to be prepared to give up our priorities, our self-interest, even our
lives, so that we can live in your way.
Help us to live your gospel, to invest in your larger future, and
discover the joy of your rule and reign.

(323) Prayer of Dedication

Lord of creation, accept our gifts as our investment in your life.
Lord of life, use us as your instruments of peace in a violent world.
Lord of love, lead us in the way of the cross, so that we may
discover your way of resurrection.

(324) Prayer of Dismissal

Let us go to face the insults and selfishness of the world.
Let us go to face ridicule and offence.
Let us to go speak out against injustice and oppression.
Let us go in the name of Jesus Christ to proclaim and to stand for the reign of God. By God's grace may we enable others to offer their hope for the future of all creation:
Let us go in peace.

SUNDAY BETWEEN 4 AND 10 SEPTEMBER INCLUSIVE

(Twenty-third Sunday in Ordinary Time)

Exodus 12.1–14 and Psalm 149 *or* Ezekiel 33.7–11
and Psalm 119.33–40; Romans 13.8–14; Matthew 18.15–20

FREEDOM IN FORGIVING

Presentation
*Illustration: blackboard/whiteboard with chalk/pen and eraser.
Using these materials, list, in general terms, sins for which people
wish to be forgiven. Demonstrate how they can be wiped away
completely. This is how completely God's love and grace towards us
releases us from the power of sin, guilt and destruction. But does this
release us from obligations towards those around us, especially those
against whom we have sinned? What scars and burdens do we continue to carry? How should we use the freedom we have been given?*

(325) Call to Worship

Psalm 149.1–4 *or* Psalm 119.33–35, 39–40, *or the following:*

Praise the Lord!
Sing a new song to the Lord!
Sing praise, all the people of God!
Let us rejoice in God,
for God delights in us.
Let us praise our God with dancing:
Play drums and harps in praise!

(326) Prayer of Adoration

Father God, as we gather in your presence,
we give thanks
– for the guarding of your Spirit, which means that we do not have
  to give in to temptation.
– for the watchfulness of your healing care, which touches each
  part of our lives with forgiveness.
– for your vigilance, which strengthens us in our fight with evil.
Lead us into a new freedom, so that we may be always alert to
serve you, offering the liberty of your love to all we meet.

(327) Prayer of Confession

The first three sections of this prayer could be taken by three different voices. The fourth section should be taken by the one leading worship. The prayer could be concluded with a further silence and the Meditation which follows.

Is it really possible, to have our guilt taken away?
Can we be forgiven, does it work?
What about all the things I have said and done?
– those things that hurt, that deceived?
– those secret thoughts known only to you?
Can I be forgiven?
Silence.

I can't believe it!
For so long I have turned my back on God and have gone my own
     way.
I have looked after myself and ignored the needs of others.
But now you are coming with open arms to receive me.
I feel your closeness, your warmth, your comfort, your love
surrounding me, enveloping me: I am no longer my own but yours!
Silence.

Forgiveness is hard work!
I want to forgive, but he won't listen.
We want to forgive but they keep ignoring us.
How can she make him understand that she is serious, that she
really is offering him a new chance, a clean slate, a fresh start?
Forgiveness is hard work, Lord; but we can never give up, for
forgiveness gives reality to our hope.
Silence.

Forgiving God,
you have mercy on us when we turn again to you.
You declare us forgiven, you proclaim us free.
Grant us the confidence to believe it, the grace to receive it,
and the courage to work out what this means for us and for others.

(328) Meditation

This reflection could follow the prayer of confession, or the reading of Romans 13.8–14.

Take up the weapons of the Lord Jesus Christ.
What are your weapons, O Lord?
Are they weapons of defence or of attack?
What are these I see before me?
– a bowl and towel,
– a plate and a cup,
– an empty cross and a door open to the world.

(329) Prayer of Dismissal

Go, for you are free.
Go, for you have Good News to share.
Go, in the name of Jesus who is ahead of us preparing the way.
Go, in the name of the Creator who is making all things new.
Go, in the power of the Spirit, who frees us to serve.

SUNDAY BETWEEN 11 AND 17 SEPTEMBER INCLUSIVE

(Twenty-fourth Sunday in Ordinary Time)

Exodus 14.19–31 and Psalm 114
(*or* Canticle: Exodus 15.1b–11, 20–21) or Genesis 50.15–21
and Psalm 103.(1–7) 8–13; Romans 14.1–12; Matthew 18.21–35

LOVE NEVER ENDS

Presentation

Illustration: paintbrush/paintpot for 'painting the Forth Bridge'. Discuss the meaning of this metaphor, that certain tasks are or seem to be endless, no sooner done than they must be done again. Think about types of work – especially those which involve caring for people – which have no clear boundary, so that we rarely feel that we have finished, or even 'done enough'. Do we agree that in relationships 'there is always something more which can be done'? Does this endlessness of loving feel creative or just relentlessly demanding? How can we help each other with the work of loving others that knows no end? How does God's endless love for us help us to bear with others?

(330) Call to Worship

Psalm 114.7–8 *or* Exodus 15.2 *or* Psalm 103.1–2, *or the following:*

(331) Prayer of Adoration

Sing to the Lord who is love!
Sing to the Lord who is glory!
**The Lord is our strength and our song
and has become our saving help.**

Who can be compared with you, O loving God?
For you are splendid in majesty, awesome in purity, the worker of wonders:
**The Lord is our strength and our song
and has become our saving help.**

163

In your steadfast love you have saved us from evil, led us out of
danger, and strengthened us for our journey to your holy place:
**The Lord is our strength and our song and has become our
saving help.**

You have gathered us and planted us as your garden
as your own people to celebrate your love
and rejoice in all that you have done:
**The Lord is our strength and our song
and has become our saving help.**

(332) Prayer of Confession

Loving King, we bring our debts to your house,
and pray that you will answer us with forgiveness.
You have given us treasures of love and peace,
opportunity and joy, knowledge and honesty.
But we have been poor stewards of your gifts,
and have not loved them, nor used them, as we ought.

So now we bring debts of selfishness,
of greed and thoughtlessness, prejudice and obstinacy,
pride and deceit.
We fall on our knees and look into your face,
where we see love, peace, joy,
knowledge, honesty, compassion.
God of grace, forgive us our debts,
as we forgive others who owe debts to us.
Silence. Psalm 103.8–13 may be read.

The Creator loves all that is made,
the Saviour forgives all our debts,
the Spirit showers new treasures around us.
Our one, holy God, loves us to freedom, today and forever.

(333) Prayer of Thanksgiving

God of love, you bear all things.
You have carried our sin on the cross:
Lead us onward into love.

God of love, there is no limit to your faith in us.
You have kept faith with us even when we failed you:
Lead us onward into love.

God of love, yours is a boundless hope.
You have woven a dream of peace for all people:
Lead us onward into love.

God of love, you endure all things.
You have reached beyond our disobedience to build a community
of justice:
Lead us onward into love.

God of love, your love never ends.
As we believe in you and hope in you,
may we learn how to bear the burdens of others,
and endure the pain of sacrifice
that your love may be made real throughout the world.

(334) Prayer of Dedication

Generous God,
we bring the gifts that you have given us.
We would love the people you have given us.
We would serve the world that you have given us.
We call your blessing upon us all,
and all that we bring in Christ.

(335) Prayer of Dismissal

Go into the unlimited love of God:
to be carried by a generous compassion,
as servants of unending grace.

SUNDAY BETWEEN 18 AND 24 SEPTEMBER INCLUSIVE

(Twenty-fifth Sunday in Ordinary Time)

Exodus 16.2–15 and Psalm 105.1–6, 37–45 *or* Jonah 3.10–4.11 and Psalm 145.1–8; Philippians 1.21–30; Matthew 20.1–16

IT'S NOT FAIR!

Presentation
Illustration: unequal tasks but equal rewards. Set tasks for two groups of volunteers. For the first group ensure that the task is much greater than the task given to the second group, but give both groups the same reward, e.g. of sweets. Is that fair? Reflect on how God's generosity often seems unfair because it seems to ask more of us than is reasonable, or because those who offer most receive no more than those who make their offering late or grudgingly. Draw out the fact that this unfairness comes from our seeing our offering as the priority, whereas God's love sees the need of the person as the priority. If God loves a cheerful giver, what does this imply about our attitude to those who offer less than we do?

(336) Call to Worship

Psalm 105.1–3 *or* 1–4; *or* Psalm 145.1–3 *or* 1–4.

(337) Prayer of Adoration and Acknowledgment

Glad and generous God,
draw us into the outpouring of your love,
that we may not begrudge your grace.
For you feed the hungry
   whether or not they have worked for it;
you forgive those who repent
   whether or not they have been adequately punished;
you provide a welcome for the stranger
   whether or not they are nice to know;
you give life to all people
whether or not they use it well.
Silence.

Glad and generous God,
forgive our resentment at the liberality of your blessings,
the profusion of gifts poured out on good and bad alike,
the abundance of your mercy, on which we too depend:
Draw us into the flow of your compassion,
that we may not resist the healing tide of grace.

(338) Prayer of Thanksgiving

My heart sings praise to my God,
for in God I find mercy and peace,
kindness and forgiveness, understanding and encouragement.
Lift up your hearts:
We lift them to the Lord.

The heart of my family sings praise to God,
the Father and Mother of all:
for in God we find joy and security,
wisdom and honesty, strength and stability.
Lift up your hearts:
We lift them to the Lord.

The heart of our community sings praise to God,
the life of our time:
for in God we find loyalty and respect,
a listener and a protector, guidance and hope.
Lift up your hearts:
We lift them to the Lord.

The heart of our world sings praise to God,
the almighty ruler:
for in God we find the past understood,
the present given hope, the future offered.
Lift up your hearts:
We lift them to the Lord.

(339) Meditation

I am at work in your field, O Lord, and my back, my head, my arms,
my fingers ache with the effort. Reaching to pick each grape of life
takes its toll on my body. I look to my right and see those who are in
the field with their parents, bringing in your harvest in each
generation; and I wonder if my children will harvest with me. I look
to my left and see a child newly reaching towards your vine,

stretching for each sweet fruit with new passion and energy and need; and I wonder if I could find that energy ever again. I look at my fingers, stretched and stained, as if with blood, and I wonder if my pickings will be what you desire.

(340) Prayer of Dedication

O God of all grace,
we find in you an awesome generosity;
your rain falls on the just and the unjust,
your mercy provides bread in the desert,
your joy gives nourishment for growth,
and food for a feast.

What can we offer to you? Yet you ask of us!
What can we do for you? Yet you call us to follow!

May we make our offering with hands that are open,
and hearts that are not closed up with resentment.
May there be no spirit of murmuring amongst us,
but may our giving be focussed on the needs of others,
not in the pride – or cost – of our gift.

For your love is turning our world inside out
as we learn to treasure all that Jesus has given us
    and given for us;
and your justice is turning our world upside down
as we honour the last and the least
    for his sake.

(341) Prayer of Dismissal

Go with God, who will provide for you with an open hand, and cherish you with an open heart.
Go with God, who calls you to be bearers of the divine generosity in the parched and starving places of the world.

SUNDAY BETWEEN
25 SEPTEMBER AND 1 OCTOBER
INCLUSIVE

(Twenty-sixth Sunday in Ordinary Time)

Exodus 17.1–7 and Psalm 78.1–4, 12–16 *or* Ezekiel 18.1–4, 25–32
and Psalm 25.1–9; Philippians 2.1–13; Matthew 21.23–32

SAYS WHO?

Presentation
*Illustration: 'authority figures'. Use symbols to illustrate different
sources of authority, such as the Bible, parents and grandparents,
teachers, the aristocracy, government, the police, clergy, person of
high rank in the armed forces etc. Using personal experience – or by
interview with an 'authority figure' – reflect on the way our response
to authority has changed in this century. What are the positive
aspects of this (e.g. greater social equality and mobility, greater
personal freedom, greater emphasis on consensus and consent).
What are the drawbacks (e.g. sense of lawlessness and outbreaks of
violent disorder, abuse towards and physical attacks on teachers,
social workers, police etc., fear and uncertainty amongst the elderly,
women and other social groups). From where did Jesus derive his
authority, and might his life offer us pointers as to the quality of
authority we should be encouraging in each other, and in the
church?*

(342) Call to Worship

Psalm 78.1–4, *or* Psalm 25.4–6

(343) Prayer of Adoration

Father-Mother God, you give us life in generosity and freedom:
We adore you.
Lord of glory, you have died in utmost compassion for us:
We adore you.
Spirit of knowledge and power, you will lead us in the way of
humble self-giving:
We adore you.

(344) Prayer of Confession

We bring to our almighty and perfect God the shortcomings of our lives, the frailties of our days, the disappointments of our hearts. We admit and confess our sins in the hearing of our loving God, and in the presence of our family of faith.

We come to the Lord with the burden of our own sins: selfishness, stubbornness, willfulness, pride, greed, envy, malice, insensitivity, cruelty.
Silence.

The Lord says: Come to me, all who are tired by heavy loads:
And I will give you rest.

We come to the Lord with the burden of the sins of our community: neglect, loneliness, derision, poverty, prejudice.
Silence.

The Lord says: Come to me, all who are tired by heavy loads:
And I will give you rest.

We come to the Lord with the burden of the sins of the whole world: the abuse of power, warfare, famine, torture, injustice.
Silence.

The Lord says: Come to me, all who are tired by heavy loads:
And I will give you rest.

Precious Lord, we hear your voice and trust in your coming peace. We rely on your strength, and promise our co-operation. We know your love, and look toward holiness in you.

(345) Prayer of Thanksgiving

Father-Mother God, you take no pleasure in the death of your children. You call us to life and freedom:
We give you thanks and praise.
Lord of glory, you spent yourself in compassion toward all who came to you, and you love us still:
We give you thanks and praise.
Spirit of holiness, you pour out your life in our hearts to quench our thirst for renewal, and to refresh us for service:
We give you thanks and praise.

(346) Prayer of Petition

Sovereign God, we want to serve you:
Teach us to be obedient.
Healing Saviour, we want to keep faith with you:
Teach us to honour you in everything we do.
Gracious Spirit, we want to receive you:
Teach us to welcome your lessons in what it means to love.

(347) Prayer of Dedication or Dismissal

In thanks for your grace, we praise you, Creator God.
In thanks for your humility, we praise you, Saviour Christ.
In thanks for your abundant blessing, we praise you, generous
  Spirit.
In thanks for your healing love at work in our midst,
we have served you in our worship; we will live for you in joy.

SUNDAY BETWEEN 2 AND 8 OCTOBER INCLUSIVE

(Twenty-seventh Sunday in Ordinary Time)

Exodus 20.1–4, 7–9, 12–20 and Psalm 19 *or* Isaiah 5.1–7 and Psalm 80.7–15; Philippians 3.4b-14; Matthew 21.33–46

DON'T CARE, WON'T CARE

Presentation
Illustration: glossy adverts for luxury cars, perfume, clothes etc. What kind of lifestyle are such adverts selling? Does it presuppose a life centred on God, on the needs of my neighbour, or on myself? How do we decide between what we want and what we need? What are the priorities of a God-centred life, and how do these differ from those of a me-centred one? What are the attitudes and assumptions which lead us to think that we can 'claim the vineyard' for ourselves – that we can go for anything we can get, regardless of how we acquire it, or what effect this has on other people?

(348) Call to Worship

Exodus 20.1–3, *or* Psalm 19.1–4, *or* Psalm 80.7, 14–15, 19; *or the following:*

Let us praise God for the wonderful care
which goes with us day by day:
Let us give thanks to God!
Let us praise God for the nurturing love
which strengthens us on the way:
Let us give thanks to God!
Let us praise God for the nourishing grace
which provides for our every need:
Let us give thanks to God!
Let us praise God for forgiving our sins
that we may be free indeed:
Let us give thanks to God!

(349) Prayer of Adoration

O Mighty King,
your crystal heavens shine upon us the light of your glory:
every night you enfold us with the comfort of your love.
Each new morning you surround us with the freshness of your
    grace.
Without words you speak of your love for the world,
in timeless silences of beauty and hope.
You are Alpha and Omega, sunrise and sunset,
the birth and rebirth of the world.
You meet us in the morning as the dew on the grass.
You nourish us as the corn of the field.
You treasure us as the apple of your eye.

Though we run from your presence, and are afraid to be loved,
yet in your time
your light shines in every corner, and your peace stills every storm.

*Your breath is the life of all living,
your words are perfect, fulfilling, complete:
a staff to the frail, a guide to the lost, wisdom to the world.
We offer hearts and lives in praise and prayer
for we know you to be our God.
Hear us, see us, touch us, O friend and King;
receive our gifts of praise and need, and meet us in this hour.

*This paragraph could be used – or repeated – as a Prayer of
Dismissal*

Prayers of Confession

(350)

Read Exodus 20.1–4.
God of deliverance,
we have been ungrateful for the freedom you have given us,
failing to put you first in our lives,
and preferring to make our own gods from material things.
Forgive us, merciful God:
That we may be renewed in holiness and grace.

Read Exodus 20.7–9.
O God of truth,
we have tried to deceive you, each other, and ourselves,
resisting your discipline of grace,
reluctant to devote ourselves to your creative glory.
Forgive us, merciful God:
That we may be renewed in holiness and grace.

Read Exodus 20.12–20.
O God of love,
we have not lived in reverence, compassion and mercy
with our families, our neighbours or your world.
We have lost our awe of you, of creation, of life itself.
Forgive us, merciful God:
That we may be renewed in holiness and grace.

Speak to our trembling hearts, holy God,
that we may be renewed through hearing your word,
and live out your purposes in wisdom, carefulness and joy.

(351)

Read Isaiah 5.7.
Merciful God, we confess
that we have not remained true to your purpose for us.
We have spoiled your pleasant planting with our arrogance and
    obstinacy.
We have not yielded the fruit of your asking,
but have followed our own path of rebellion and deceit.
We have allowed the briars of hatred and the thorns of violence to
    grow unhindered in our midst.
Forgive us, God of mercy:
Hear and heal us, restore and renew us,
that we may once again grow true to your intention,
and live to your praise and glory.

(352) Prayer of Dedication

Call us, God of steadfast love,
out of the stress and fear of the world
into the vineyard of your peace:
Call us into life.

Come to us, God of light and hope,
as we struggle with conflict and difficulty,
and lead us into a deeper compassion:
Call us into life.

Walk with us, God of strength and song,
along your way of generous grace,
that as we journey through creation
deserts may be transformed into gardens of fruitfulness:
Call us into life.

(353) Prayer of Dismissal

Go into the vineyard of God,
not as its conquerors but as servants of all whom you find there.
Go into the vineyard to discover God who is the gardener,
renewing Eden throughout the earth.

SUNDAY BETWEEN 9 AND 15 OCTOBER INCLUSIVE

(Twenty-eighth Sunday in Ordinary Time)

Exodus 32.1–14 and Psalm 106.1–6, 19–23 *or* Isaiah 25.1–9 and Psalm 23; Philippians 4. 1–9; Matthew 22.1–14

COUNT ME IN!

Presentation

Illustration: an invitation to a party or wedding. What are the characteristics of a good party? Make a list and grade them in order of importance. What kind of attitude and behaviour do we hope for in party guests? Should we welcome any excuse for a party, or should we consider what is being celebrated (e.g. Exodus 32. 1–14) Reflect on God's desire for us to share the divine presence and joy. Do we find it easy to imagine or believe that God rejoices in us, takes pleasure in us, delights in our company? If church is a good party where everyone enjoys being together, how might this help – or hinder – our mission?

(354) Call to Worship

Psalm 106. 1–3 *or* Isaiah 25.1, 6–7.

✤ (355) Prayer of Adoration, Confession and Thanksgiving

We come, O King, to your feast,
invited by your Son, Jesus our Lord.
We have brought the worries of our days with us;
we have brought those we love with us, in our hearts,
we have brought the burdens of our wrong-doing,
we have brought our offerings for the feast.
We are, each one, both sinner and saint.
We come, O King, to your feast,
invited by your Son, Jesus our Lord.
Silence.

We come, O King, but we come reluctantly.
When your word challenged us, we found other things to do.
When your messenger called us, we made excuses.
We have not sought the loveliness of your life,

the beauty of your love, the joy of your presence.
We have not followed our highest and best desires.
We have begrudged the time, the energy, the commitment;
denied you the pleasure of our company;
refused the gift of ourselves.
Silence.

Thank you, royal God,
that you continue to invite us to your feast,
that you are happy to fill your hall with all manner of people;
for here we find that we can feel at home.
You love us, and you want us to be here.

(356) Prayer of Petition and Thanksgiving

In an age of pain, we wait to hear the voices of those who cry out
to God, and we affirm our faith that God hears and answers their
plea.
Silence.

We have waited for God and we have been saved:
Let us rejoice and be glad.

In a time of poverty, when people starve for land, for hope, for
justice and for bread, let us be silent before God.
Silence.

We have waited for God and we have been saved:
Let us rejoice and be glad.

In a time of violence, when peoples and nations are torn apart by
ancient anger and modern technology, let us be silent before God.
Silence.

We have waited for God and we have been saved:
Let us rejoice and be glad.

In a time of reproach, when the faith of our forebears is despised,
and our own faith is mocked, belittled and ignored, let us be silent
before God.
Silence.

We have waited for God and we have been saved:
Let us rejoice and be glad.

In this time of poverty, violence and reproach, let us continue to hold before God those who suffer, trusting that God's blessing will fall on all who cry out in distress.
Silence.

We have waited for God and we have been saved:
Let us rejoice and be glad.

(357) Prayer of Dedication and Dismissal

As we go into places of suffering,
may your love wipe all tears away.
As we go into places of hunger,
may your love give bread and hope.
As we go into places of fear,
may your love provide peace and companionship.
As we go into your world,
may your love speak of grace,
and sing of joy:
Loving God, grant us the courage to go
where you would send us.

SUNDAY BETWEEN 16 AND 22 OCTOBER INCLUSIVE

(Twenty-ninth Sunday in Ordinary Time)

Exodus 33.12–23 and Psalm 99, *or*
Isaiah 45.1–7 and Psalm 96.1–9 (10–13);
I Thessalonians 1.1–10; Matthew 22.15–22

WHOM DO YOU SERVE?

Presentation

*Illustration: coins and banknotes. Whose head is on our coin?
What taxes do we pay with such coins, and why? How does this
illustrate our loyalty to, and service of, our country? Under what
circumstances might we become less willing to pay our taxes? If we
were to engage in such 'civil disobedience' is this simply serving our
own ends, or would we consider ourselves to be serving a greater
cause?*

(358) Call to Worship

Psalm 96.1–3, or 1–6, *or the following:*

Holy is the Lord our God:
The Lord our God is holy.
Holy is the Lord our King:
The Lord our God is holy.
Holy is our God who reigns:
The Lord our God is holy.
Holy in justice, holy in peace:
The Lord our God is holy.

(359) Prayer of Adoration

God of majesty, as we come to worship you
it is as though we are standing with Moses on the holy mountain;
or with David on the City of Zion;
or with the prophets and saints in your heavenly court:
Sing to God a new song!
Sing to God all the earth!
Praise the holy name of the Lord!

As we come into your presence,
it is as though we join with the Israelites
bringing their offerings in procession
with psalms and hymns and trumpets.
singing with joy of the beauty that we find here in your sanctuary:
Sing to God a new song!
Sing to God all the earth!
Praise the holy name of the Lord!

God in majesty, all the wise cry out to you in their need,
and we want to tell all the world of your marvels,
your wonders and your care.
We come to declare your justice, to proclaim that your love
is the firm foundation of our lives:
Sing to God a new song!
Sing to God all the earth!
Praise the holy name of the Lord!

(360) Prayer of Confession

God of truth, you are searching for truth in us,
for that wholehearted devotion which takes up all we are
and turns it towards your purpose and your ways.
Silence.

That we may serve the living God:
And await the One who saves us.

God of truth, help us to turn away from all that is false in us and in
the world, all that is hypocritical and insincere.
Help us to turn aside from any loyalty which stands between ourselves
and you, that our service to you may be complete, pure, holy.
Silence.

That we may serve the living God:
And await the One who saves us.

God of truth, you look for obedience and faithfulness in us,
a standard of integrity which comes from the heart,
and which shows where our true loyalty lies.
You expect us to strive for this in ourselves,
and honour it in each other.
Silence.

That we may serve the living God:
And await the One who saves us.

(361) Prayer of Thanksgiving

Pilgrim God, we praise you for that grace which is always on the
move from death to life, desolation to hope, famine to feasting.
As we travel this road of pain and rejoicing, we give thanks that
you go with us as our guardian and friend:
– that you have taken us by the hand and led us,
  giving guidance and support.
  Your presence travels with us: **You will give us rest.**
– that you have strengthened us for the work of faith,
  the labour of love, the steadfastness of hope.
  Your presence travels with us: **You will give us rest.**
– that you have made us imitators of your saints and disciples,
  and of our Saviour, our Lord Jesus Christ.
  Your presence travels with us: **You will give us rest.**
– that as we have received your Word with joy,
  even in the midst of our suffering, you have revealed to us your
    ways.
  Your presence travels with us: **You will give us rest.**
– that we belong to you and you have shown us your glory.
  Your presence travels with us: **You will give us rest.**
– that through our example others have been encouraged and
    inspired.
  Your presence travels with us: **You will give us rest.**

(362) Prayer of Dedication

O God of mystery, awesome and unknown,
you bind all creation together in purpose and potential.
Beside you, all powers are weak and helpless.
Apart from you, we have no strength.
Beyond you, there is nothing, whether created or uncreated.
  To God alone be all glory:
  To God alone be all praise.

As you hid Moses in the cleft of rock, so you hide us in your loving
grace, that we may not be destroyed by your wrath or overwhelmed
by your majesty.
  To God alone be all glory:
  To God alone be all praise.

Like our fathers and mothers in faith, we find that you go before us, clearing the road, opening the way, dividing the sea of indifference, levelling the mountains of hate.

To God alone be all glory:
To God alone be all praise.

With the prophets and teachers of the past, we search the scriptures by your Holy Spirit, understanding what you reveal to us, asking that you will show us more, craving the treasures that are hidden there, the unwanted hoards of your wisdom.

To God alone be all glory:
To God alone be all praise.

And as others have discovered, we too find you caring for those who do not know you; calling them by name, commissioning them in their work, for none of us travel for ourselves alone. They, and we, are called for the sake of those we can serve.

To God alone be all glory:
To God alone be all praise.

O God of mystery, awesome and unknown,
you form light and darkness, create both wealth and woe. In you all the heights and depths that lie beyond us are held, carried and redeemed to form one treasury of joy and life abundant, in time and in eternity:

To God alone be all glory:
To God alone be all praise.

(363) Prayer of Dismissal

Go out in peace, to serve the holy God
in love and justice, through sacrifice, always in praise:
God of glory, come to us.
God of glory, stay with us.
God of glory, travel with us.
God of glory, lead us home.

SUNDAY BETWEEN 23 AND 29 OCTOBER INCLUSIVE

(Thirtieth Sunday in Ordinary Time)

Deuteronomy 34.1–12 and Psalm 90.1–6, 13–17
or Leviticus 19.1–2, 15–18 and Psalm 1; I Thessalonians 2.1–8;
Matthew 22.34–46

PROMISED LAND

Presentation
Illustration: earth and water, bricks and bread, a flowering plant and a child (or a picture of one). Discuss the dream of a 'Promised Land': what kind of dream did the Israelites have of the land towards which God was leading them? What dreams might we have of a 'Promised Land' for ourselves or our children? What are the ingredients of our dream? Land (earth and water); food and shelter (bricks and bread); relationships between people, and with the environment (plant and child)? Do our hopes include all of these, a combination of them – or are they less specific? Does the 'Promised Land' have to 'get real' in our everyday world, or does it always lie ahead of us?

(364) Call to Worship

Psalm 90.1–2 *or* Matthew 22.37–39.

(365) Prayer of Adoration

O God of our life: **We love you.**
O God of all truth: **We adore you.**
O God of steadfast love: **We gather to sing your praise.**

As we pray and read your word,
we grow in strength and holiness,
like a tree that is planted beside a stream of pure water.
As the tree draws in moisture and goodness through its roots,
we draw in food for the good life you have promised us.
As each leaf of the tree becomes fresh and green,
and each bud blossoms into flower and fruit,
so we are renewed and blessed by your strength flowing through us.

O God of our life: **We love you.**
O God of all truth: **We adore you.**
O God of steadfast love: **We gather to sing your praise.**

(366) Prayer of Confession

Holy God, we confess that we have not loved you
with all our heart, mind, soul and strength.
Loving God, forgive us: **Make us holy, for you are all holiness.**

Holy God, we confess that we have not loved our neighbour
as we love ourselves, and as we hope to be loved.
Loving God, forgive us: **Make us holy, for you are all holiness.**

Holy God, we confess that we collude with a society
in which there is little reverence for the values of the kingdom.
Loving God, forgive us: **Make us holy, for you are all holiness.**

Holy God, we confess that we are too comfortable with a world
in which the poor are exploited and the destitute starved.
Loving God, forgive us: **Make us holy, for you are all holiness.**

Holy God, we confess that we have worshipped the false gods
of power and superiority, of success and status and conquest.
Loving God, forgive us: **Make us holy, for you are all holiness.**

(367) Prayer of Thanksgiving

God before creation: you are the maker of all that is.
In your presence all human power falls to nothing.
fading and failing into turmoil and trouble.

God before time: you are the first and the last.
In your presence all human life is like the blink of an eye,
generation after generation unfolding in your sight.

God before history: you are the one who sees and knows.
In your presence nothing is hidden, all secrets are searched out,
everything is tested, and both good and bad are judged for what
  they are.

God has entered creation, time and history as a human being.
In your presence we love you, ask of you, and live to serve you,
sharing your grace in all your work,
sharing your grace with all the world.
Silence. Psalm 90.13–17 may be read.

(368) Prayer of Dedication

Creator God, Lord of the far horizon,
you have given us a glimpse of the promised land:
a country large enough for all the peoples of the earth;
a nation of citizens where every person finds home and peace;
a time of feasting for each human soul; plenty for all and to spare.

Thank you, loving Lord,
that in your vision everyone finds a place, a welcome and a
    blessing.
And though we cannot yet see this dream made real on earth, grant
us the courage to hope, the faith to imagine it into being,
and the love which will give what it costs to pray
'Thy kingdom come!'

(369) Prayer of Dismissal

May God who is all love, teach you all loving.
May God who is all peace, give you hope in all circumstances.
May God who is over all, call you to a larger future.
May God who is beyond all, lead you into glory.

ALL SAINTS (1 NOVEMBER)

Revelation 7.9–17; Psalm 34.1–10, 22; I John 3.1–3; Matthew 5.1–12

LET THE LIGHT SHINE THROUGH

Presentation
Illustration:stained glass windows. If a real window is not available,
display a picture of one, or mock-up your own using tissue paper
mounted in a frame of black card. Or project a slide transparency on
to a screen. As we look at such a window, what do we see? Explain
the way in which the light must be allowed to pass through the glass,
and link this with the comment of a child that 'saints are people who
let the light shine through'. How do we let God's light shine through
us? As we do so, what do we reveal of God – and of ourselves?

(370) Call to Worship

Psalm 34.1–3.

(371) Prayer of Adoration

This prayer could follow the reading from Revelation 7.9–17.

Glorious God, with the great crowd of peoples gathered in your
presence, we give our adoration:
Blessing and glory and honour and praise
be yours forever and ever!

With angels and elders and mysterious creatures, we offer our
worship:
Blessing and glory and honour and praise
be yours forever and ever!

With all tribes and nations and people from every race and tongue,
we sing out our love:
Blessing and glory and honour and praise
be yours forever and ever!

With all those whose suffering has brought them close to Christ,
we serve through the sacrifice of praise:
Blessing and glory and honour and praise
be yours forever and ever!

With all whom you have called, all whom you have loved,
and all who will one day bow before your throne,
we celebrate your saving grace:
**Blessing and glory and honour and praise
be yours forever and ever!**

(372) Prayer of Acknowledgment and Thanksgiving

*This prayer could follow the reading of I John 3.1–3. Psalm 34.8
could be used as a refrain, spoken by a second voice, or the
congregation.*

O God of love, you are transforming us through love.
We cried to you, and you listened,
saving us from the depths of our trouble.
We searched for you, and you found us,
we are surrounded by your steadfast love.
Refrain.

We disowned you, yet you claimed us,
putting your name on us, recreating us as your own.
We came to you in fear, and you set us free,
so that we need never feel ashamed that we serve you.
Refrain.

We are dragged down by our failures, our faults and our sins,
but you purify, heal and renew the life within us.
We are discouraged by the pain in us and in the world,
but you awaken our hearts to the fullness of your grace.
Refrain.

*O God of love, transforming us in love,
and revealing love through us to all people,
let your light shine through our prayers and words and deeds,
that the image of Christ may be the radiance in our lives
to the glory of your name.

** This paragraph could be used – or repeated – as a Prayer of
Dismissal.*

(373) Meditation

Read Hebrews 4.16.

In the heart of the Throne there is the breath of the mountain
where love comes down in teaching and instruction,
dreams come true in flesh and blood,
and we know ourselves accepted and acceptable,
blessed with the abundance provided by love.

In the heart of the Throne there is suffering.
You come to us as a sorrowing God,
stripped of power and dignity, willing to hunger and thirst with us.
What we shall be is not yet revealed,
but we shall be like Christ, for we are being re-made in his image,
cleansed towards his purity. By blood. Through sacrifice.

In the heart of the Throne there is offering.
The light of the high places – wise and gracious and beautiful –
questions our comforts and challenges our complacency.
Your prayer is our argument and inspiration;
regulating passion, directing energy,
empowering our zeal for justice.

In the heart of the Throne there is a cross-shaped void:
space for the renewal of the world.

(374) Prayer of Thanksgiving

Father of all grace, you love us.
Love is our identity.
Love makes us recognizable as your children.
Love shelters us, shepherds us, and makes us feel secure.
We are made whole in your presence – holy, complete, fulfilled.
Loving God, you call us to be your children:
Your children lack nothing that is good.

Compassionate Saviour, you love us.
You know the poverty of our spirit; the need of our souls;
the turmoil of our emotions; our weakness, frailty, doubt.
We are made whole through your generosity;
your springs of living water wash away all tears.
Loving God, you call us to be your children:
Your children lack nothing that is good.

Healing Spirit, you love us.
You absorb hatred without returning it,
receiving the conflict and transforming it into peace.
We are made whole through your offering;
as we enter the violence of others, bearing their pain for your sake,
your energy for change is released into the world.
Loving God, you call us to be your children:
Your children lack nothing that is good.

(375) Prayer of Dedication

Living God, may your grace shine through those humble hands
which, receiving your gifts with gratitude, offer them again in
sharing for the daily, hourly, feeding of the world.

SUNDAY BETWEEN 30 OCTOBER AND 5 NOVEMBER INCLUSIVE

(Thirty-first Sunday in Ordinary Time)

Joshua 3.7–17 and Psalm 107.1–7, 33–37 *or* Micah 3.5–12
and Psalm 43; I Thessalonians 2.9–13; Matthew 23.1–12 (or 24.1–14)

KEEPING ON KEEPING ON

Presentation
*Illustration: acts of endurance and persistence. What are the
qualities in a character which strengthen us to 'keep on keeping
on' in the face of opposition, threat or uncertainty? How might
we encourage such qualities in each other and 'keep each other
going' when times get tough? Are there dangers which must be
avoided?*

(376) Call to Worship

Psalm 107.1–3 or Psalm 43.3–4, *or the following:*

Let us give thanks to our God of love:
For the love of God is ours forever.
Let us give thanks that we are set free:
For the love of God is ours forever.
Let us give thanks for the blessings of life:
For the love of God is ours forever.

(377) Prayer of Adoration

God of the universe,
as your light travels across the cosmos from distant stars,
so your love reaches out to us wherever we wander,
hungry and thirsty, astray in the wilderness.

As your light is a guide in unfamiliar places,
so your love is a comfort in our distress,
releasing us from imprisonment, leading us to safety,
gathering us in security, plenty and peace.

As your light marks our passage through day and night:
each day, the fresh promise of dawn,
each year, the circle of the seasons;
so your love endures with us and for us,
bearing our need with patience,
sharing our prosperity with joy.

(378) Prayer of Confession

Father God, we appeal to your mercy.
For the times when we have laid burdens on others,
and not offered to relieve them of their load:
Father forgive us.
For the times when we have lived out our faith
so as to be seen and commended:
Father forgive us.
For the times when we have sought public gratitude
and craved acknowledgment beyond our due:
Father forgive us.
For the times when we have preferred status to servanthood,
and resented our lowly place in your community:
Father forgive us.
For the times when we have been impatient with ourselves,
each other, your church and with you:
Father forgive us.
For the times when we have looked to you for solutions
as a way of avoiding our responsibilities here and now:
Father forgive us.

(379) Prayer of Thanksgiving

Thank you, God our strength,
for the courage which keeps us going,
even when we are afraid:
We give you thanks and praise.

Thank you, God of faith,
for the trust which enables us to step out,
even when we cannot see the way:
We give you thanks and praise.

Thank you, God of compassion,
for the love that emboldens us to serve others,
even when we are bowed down by caring:
We give you thanks and praise.

Thank you, God of hope,
for the peace which guides and prompts, and reassures us,
even in the midst of grief and trouble:
We give you thanks and praise.

(380) Prayer of Petition

God of faith and courage, stay with us
in the trials and testing-places of our daily lives.
May we:
– obey your commands in humility, and exercise authority with
  compassion.
– listen for your guiding word, and expect your miracle of grace.
– abhor guile and flattery and greed, and resist the corruptions of
  status and power.
– offer ourselves to reconciliation, and keep going when the way
  becomes hard.
– work gently with others, and encourage them in their
  endeavours.
– be merciful in our righteousness, and blameless in our behaviour.
– become worthy of the name you place upon us, and the task you
  place in our hands.

(381) Prayer of Dedication

Lead us onward, God of grace,
that we may not be deceived by the lies of power,
nor become impatient with the humility of goodness.

Lead us on in love, God of grace,
that all our fears may be heard, believed and understood,
and through your acceptance transformed into hope.

*Lead us on in love each day, God of grace,
that we may come to your house of joy,
and find your rule and reign made real for all creation.

* *This paragraph could be used – or repeated – as a Prayer of
Dismissal*

SUNDAY BETWEEN 6 AND 12 NOVEMBER INCLUSIVE

(Thirty-second Sunday in Ordinary Time)

Joshua 24.1–3a, 14–25 and Psalm 78.1–7 *or* Wisdom of Solomon
6.12–16 and (Canticle) Wisdom of Solomon 6.17–20 *or* Amos 5.18–24
and Psalm 70; I Thessalonians 4.13–18; Matthew 25.1–13

KEEP WATCH!

Presentation

*Illustration: Being 'on the ball'. Play a party game such as 'Musical
Chairs', then discuss what helps us to play such games successfully
(knowing what to expect, being aware of what is going on around us,
the ability to react promptly). How do such qualities enable us to
'keep watch'? Share stories of vigilance (sources might be wartime
experiences, or parenting, or work in nursing, or the emergency
services). How are such qualities necessary in spiritual matters too?
How can we develop them in ourselves and each other?*

(382) Call to Worship

Psalm 78.1–4, *or* Psalm 70.1, 4; *or the following, which can be
chanted with clapping, the congregation repeating each line after
the leader. If desired, God/God's can be substituted for you/your.*

Let all who seek you rejoice and be glad!
Let all who love you sing praise to your name!
Let all who trust you appeal to your mercy!
Let all who serve you receive of your strength!

(383) Prayer of Adoration

Our one desire is to learn from you,
for you seek us, you lead us,
and your grace is multiplied to meet our need:
We adore you.

Our one desire is to love you,
in sincerity, with faithfulness,
gathering all that we are to serve you in praise:
We adore you.

Our one desire is to obey you,
in waiting, in keeping watch,
preparing to respond in the moment you call:
We adore you.

Our one desire is to be known by you,
as your people, as your children,
as the friends who know your methods and your mind:
We adore you.

Our one desire is a longing
which gathers up loving and learning,
obedience and knowledge
in the dedication of heart and hands and life:
We adore you.

Our one desire is also our hope:
for the clearing of the way and the opening of the land,
so that all may live within the justice of your promise,
this day and forever.

(384) Prayer of Confession

O God of liberty, we cry out to you
for freedom from all that imprisons us:
the pride of the soul, which causes us to deceive ourselves;
the corruption of our common values, which causes unfairness in
our dealings with each other,
the ideologies of violence which lead to injustice between peoples:
Let justice flow like endless waters,
and righteousness like a stream which never fails.

Silence. Wisdom 6.12–20 may be read.

O God of liberty, we cry out to you
that we may be believed in the radiance of your wisdom,
seek the unfolding of your righteous will,
wait for your love present in every moment,
and obey the disciplines of your grace,
that your reign may be fulfilled in every place:
Let justice flow like endless waters,
and righteousness like a stream which never fails.

(385) Prayer of Petition

In faith we pray for those who grieve,
that they may trust in your promise of a resurrection
where nothing of love is lost.
Lord, in your mercy: **Hear our prayer.**

In peace we pray for all who are distressed,
that we may encourage each other in faith,
and not give way to despair, like those who have no hope.
Lord, in your mercy: **Hear our prayer.**

In joy we pray with those who have gone before us,
that together, as one priesthood on earth and in heaven,
we may wait for the trumpet calling us
to stay with Christ forever.
Lord, in your mercy: **Hear our prayer.**

(386) Prayer of Dedication

Call us, God of the far horizon,
beyond offering to the purification of all our desires,
beyond commitment to a complete allegiance,
beyond gratitude to the sharing of your blessings,
beyond duty to an ardour of devotion,
beyond witness to the consecration of our lives:
And as we have chosen, so may we serve,
through the long day and night of our waiting,
till your hour is known.

(387) Prayer of Dismissal

O God our deliverer, guard us body, heart and soul from all that
would tempt us and turn us aside from your great love and your
high endeavour, that we may be well-prepared to serve you, and
ready when you call.

SUNDAY BETWEEN 13 AND 19 NOVEMBER INCLUSIVE

(Thirty-third Sunday in Ordinary Time)

Judges 4.1–7 and Psalm 123 *or* Zephaniah 1.7, 12–18 and Psalm 90.1–8 (9–11) 12; I Thessalonians 5.1–11; Matthew 25.14–30

TAKING RISKS IN LOVE

Presentation
Illustration: set of dice. Difference between gambling (taking a risk on chance, or on our own 'system') and the trading which the parable commends (investing the talents God gives us, in order to accrue 'interest' for the kingdom). What motivates the first? (greed, desire for something for nothing, excitement, an inability to cope with life as it is given, the need for the 'buzz' of success to compensate for some inadequacy, or as an escape). What motivates the second? (love of God, gratitude, obedience). Why is avoiding the risk not an option? (fear). Draw out the spiritual principles contained in verses 21 (of spiritual responsibility) and 29 (of spiritual growth). What security do we have? (knowledge of God's nature and investment in us – faith, hope, and love). In the end, we can take risks in obedience to God, because God takes a risk on us!

(388) Call to Worship

Psalm 123.1–2 *or* Psalm 90.1–2.

(389) Prayer of Adoration

Loving God, in this time of uncertainty,
we wait for you:
for your love is our security, and your faithfulness our hope.

In this time of anxiety,
we wait for you:
for your forgiveness is our assurance, and your promise is our life.

In this time when we are exposed to rebuke and mockery,
we wait for you:
for your compassion is our shelter, and your strength is our shield.

In this time when we are in pain,
we wait for you:
for your understanding is our guard, and your touch is our healing.

In this time when we are in danger,
we wait for you:
for your grace is the foundation on which we stand, and your mercy
is our daring.

In this time when we are hungry for your feeding,
and thirsty for your refreshment,
oppressed by a multitude of tasks and cares,
and battered by the contempt and indifference of the world,
we wait for your word, your lifted hand, your sign.
Silence.

Adventurous God,
you are present in our quietness, our waiting, our trust.
You do not take the safe or easy way,
but you lead us in your path of risky grace:
where in sacrifice we are united as your Body,
in generosity we are offered to our neighbours,
and in wisdom and courage we love our enemies,
for your sake, and for the sake of your kingdom,
this day and forever.

(390) Prayer of Confession

Sovereign God, we have failed you.
We have become so tired in your service,
so small-minded in our caring,
so afraid of the violence and hatred in the world.
You have searched out our wrongdoing
and brought our secret sins into the light:
Teach us to use the time you have given us,
so that we can grow in wisdom and holiness.

Generous God, we have failed you.
We have placed our wealth in material things,
giving glory to status and power,
and finding our security in work and achievement.
You have searched out our wrongdoing
and brought our secret sins into the light:
Teach us to use the time you have given us,
so that we can grow in wisdom and holiness.

Merciful God, we have failed you.
We have concealed your promises,
resisted your faith in others, and ourselves,
and refused your enlarging compassion.
You have searched out our wrongdoing
and brought our secret sins into the light:
Teach us to use the time you have given us,
so that we can grow in wisdom and holiness.

(391) Prayer of Thanksgiving

That you have invested your life in creation:
We thank you, humble God.
That you have poured out your love for humanity:
We thank you, humble God.
That you have given us your Son as our Saviour:
We thank you humble God.
That you have risked your all on our response:
We thank you, humble God.

(392) Prayer of Petition

May we have faith that all things are under your control, loving
God, and that even your fire burns us for our healing:
Hold us and help us, that we may trust in your grace.

May we see your secret works of compassion, and give thanks for
the hidden channels of your mercy in the world:
Hold us and help us, that we may trust in your grace.

May we welcome your surprising life, which overwhelms our
defences, breaks down our securities and sweeps us into new
forms, new understandings, new realms of faith:
Hold us and help us, that we may trust in your grace.

May we obey you in new adventures of service investing in others,
as you have invested in us, risking for others, as you have risked
for us:
Hold us and help us, that we may trust in your grace.

Prayers of Dedication

(393)

God of the universe,
you have given our enemies into our hands.
Not for our sakes, that we might be avenged,
but for your sake, that they might receive your mercy through us.
Not for our pride, that we might mock them,
but that we might forgive them with the forgiveness you have
shown towards us.
Not for our complacency, that we might forget them,
but that through listening we might understand them, and grow in
your wisdom.
Not for our triumph that we might feel satisfied with ourselves,
but for your compassion, that we might serve them.

(394)

Make us children of your grace, generous God,
willing to risk what we have received at your hand,
willing to invest your gifts in others,
faithful in small things and ready for the greater task.
Make us children of your vision, adventurous God,
that we may be alert and ready to respond to your leading,
with minds protected by hope,
hearts defended by faith, wills directed by love.

(395) Prayer of Dismissal

Live with us day by day, God of compassion,
that we may be generous to receive, generous to give:
that we may be worthy channels of your grace.

SUNDAY BETWEEN 20 AND 26 NOVEMBER INCLUSIVE

(Sunday before Advent)

Ezekiel 34.11–16, 20–24; Psalm 95.1–7a, (*or* Psalm 100);
Ephesians 1.15–23; Matthew 25.31–46

DOWN TO EARTH KING

Presentation
Illustration: items which suggest the 'ordinariness' or the routine of everyday life for yourself and/or the congregation, e.g. telephone, diary, letters from school, nappies, shopping list (the congregation could be invited to suggest others). Discuss the extent to which even a modern monarch would be familiar with these things. What does it mean for the King of Kings to be the one who hallows our routine, enjoys our company, shares our jokes, carries our burdens?

(396) Call to Worship

Psalm 95.1–2, 6–7 *or* Psalm 100.1–3, *or the following:*

Praise the Lord, all the earth!
Praise the King of all the world!
Praise the Lord, all you peoples!
Praise the King of all the nations!
Praise the Lord, great and mighty!
Praise the King who builds us up!
Praise the Lord, kind and gentle!
Praise the King who meets our needs!

(397) Prayer of Adoration

Loving God, we adore you,
Sovereign of all, we praise your holy name.
For you are our God and our King:
**We are the people of your pasture
and the sheep of your hand.**

Suffering Christ, we adore you,
Saviour of all, we praise your holy name.
For you are our God and our King:
We are the people of your pasture
and the sheep of your hand.

Joyous Spirit, we adore you,
Freedom of all, we praise your holy name.
For you are our God and our King:
We are the people of your pasture
and the sheep of your hand.

Shepherd God – our Maker, Redeemer and Friend – we adore you,
singing for joy in your presence,
worshipping you with thanksgiving,
humbling our pride with praise.
For you are our strength, our protection and our hope,
source of goodness and love, faith and healing;
and with all the earth we call out to you in gladness,
before all the world we bless you as our King:
We are the people of your pasture
and the sheep of your hand.

(398) Prayer of Acknowledgment

God of all creation,
yours are the desert and the garden, the ocean and the continent;
your love holds both the heights and the depths,
searching the hearts of all people,
calling the strayed, seeking the lost:
I will feed them with justice, says the Lord.

Your comfort reaches those who are scattered,
guides those who are confused,
heals those who are wounded,
rescues those in terror:
I will feed them with justice, says the Lord.

Your compassion travels with the exile, the wanderer, the refugee,
and with all those who live away from home,
that they may find pastures for nourishment,
and pools for refreshing,
and find you to be their strength and song,
even in a foreign land:
I will feed them with justice, says the Lord.

Your truth will search out wrongdoing,
and make a stand against oppression;
strengthening the poor, lifting up the weak,
and bringing the tyrants to judgment:
I will feed them with justice, says the Lord.

(399) Prayer of Dedication

O God of majesty,
as you have raised your Son, Jesus Christ from the dead,
and exalted him as our Saviour and Judge,
so give us life and call us to truth and compassion.

O God of glory,
as you have made your Son, Jesus Christ,
head over all things for the church,
so increase that love which recreates us as his body.

O God of mercy,
as you have offered your Son, Jesus Christ,
into the pain and hatred and grief of the world,
so keep us faithful in suffering and wise in our witness.

O God of renewal,
as you have revealed your Son, Jesus Christ,
in the person of our neighbour,
so may we offer bread for his hunger,
clothes for his nakedness, welcome for his loneliness,
and grace in all the prisons of the soul.

(400) Prayer of Dismissal

As the children of God, let us bear fruit in the lives of those around
    us.
As the household of God, let us be salt in our communities.
As the people of God, let us be light to the world.

Appendix 1 – Declarations of God's Forgiveness and Grace

The following declarations of God's love can be used at any time of the year, but some have been written to link with the specific themes of a particular season or occasion:

(401) *Advent*

God has declared a time of mercy and grace.
God has proclaimed the rule of justice and peace.
God has promised to live as love in our midst.
To God be the glory!
Thy kingdom come!

(402) *Advent/Pentecost*

The life of God is growing in us.
The holiness of Christ is purifying us.
The fruits of the Spirit are making us whole:
Praise God – we are forgiven and reborn.
Praise God – who is making all things new.

(403) *Christmas*

Good News! We are heard!
Good News! We are loved!
Good News! We are forgiven!
Good News! God is with us!
Good News! God is with us!

(404) *Christmas*

God is with us
– as the one who has heard our plea
– as the one who fulfills all promise and potential for good
– as the one who bears our burden and understands our need:
God is with us!
Praise to the living God!

(405) *Christmas*

Love has come into the world
to hear the cry of the poor,
to heal the sick and touch our need.
Love has come to set the prisoners free:
Loving God, we praise your name!

(406) *Epiphany*

The light of the world has dawned in our hearts for our forgiveness:
Thanks be to God.
The light of the world has dawned in our community for our
    healing:
Thanks be to God.
The light of the world has dawned among the nations that justice
may be done:
Thanks to God.

(407) *Covenant/Vocation*

God who is calling us into holiness
holds us in mercy as we learn to be disciples,
holds us in grace as we turn again to truth,
holds us in forgiveness as we serve in love and hope:
Keep us faithful, Holy God, keep us true.

(408) *Vocation/Unity/Pentecost*

The pilgrim God
receives us in love to be companions on the way of the Spirit
into deeper compassion, into greater grace:
Thanks be to God.

(409) *Lent/Holy Week*

God is grace – setting aside the power of heaven
to walk our road in humility and hope.
God is grace – travelling beside us
receiving our burden, bearing our load.
God is grace – we are forgiven!
God is grace – we are renewed!

(410) *Lent/Holy Week*

As one who weeps with those who weep
and laughs with those who rejoice,
God shares our anguish and our hope
and calls us onward into life:
We are loved, forgiven, free!

(411) *Lent/Holy Week*

Our loving God – the source of all blessing –
is drawing us into hope;
forgiving our sin, healing our wounds,
bearing the suffering of the world:
Thanks be to God.

(412) *Transfiguration*

God who is mystery
reveals to us the truth of Christ.
God who is compassion
forgives our failings, bears our wrong.
God who is love
calls us through death to life:
Thanks be to God.

(413) *Mothering Sunday*

Our God surrounds us with a mother's love.
Our God sustains us with a mother's care.
Our God forgives us with a mother's hope.
Our God renews us in a mother's trust:
Glory to God. Glory to God!

(414) *Easter/Pentecost*

The life of God –
stronger than our sin, stronger than evil, stronger than death –
wells up to renew us.
The love of God –
stronger than deceit, stronger than hatred, stronger than violence –
flows free to renew the world.

(415) *Easter/Pentecost*

Praise to our God who has given us life:
Praise to our God who has given us hope.
Praise to our God who has given us joy:
Praise to our God who has forgiven us!

(416)

The God of holiness, declaring us forgiven,
calls us children of hope, heirs of the promise,
salt of the earth, light to the world:
Thanks be to God.

(417)

God our Creator has heard our cry.
God our Saviour has forgiven our sins.
God our Advocate renews us in grace:
All glory and praise to God!

(418)

Into your hands we lay our wrongdoing
and from your grace receive freedom and hope.
Into your peace we lay our distress at the evil in the world
and from your grace receive wisdom and zeal.
Into your love we lay our work for your glory
and receive from your grace justice and courage:
Your kingdom come.

(419)

The God of grace forgives us.
The God of compassion receives us with love.
The God of generosity will provide for our needs.
The God of joy is glad in our company:
Thanks be to God!

Appendix 2 – Prayers for Communion

These prayers can provide a link between the overall theme of a service and the sacrament of Holy Communion. Most are written to be offered immediately prior to the sharing of bread and wine, but some can also be used after the celebration. Though written for specific seasons or occasions, they can be considered for use at other times of the year.

(420) *Advent*

Lord, as we wait for you,
    feed us with courage for the challenge of the hour.
Lord, as we wait for you,
    nourish our faith to meet the demands of the day.
Lord, as we wait for you,
    sustain us in hope that we may catch the vision of your realm
    and reign.
Lord, as we wait for you,
    come to us, living God, come.

(421) *Advent/Holy Week*

We have come to the house of the Lord.
We are gathered at his table. We are here to share the feast,
remembering that:
    You have declared the kingdom – to us
    You lived out its promises – for us
    Your strength was broken – for us
    You walked into shadow – for us
Lord, as you died for us, so we remember you now –
life given in love – and we thank you.

(422) *Advent/Holy Week*

We have eaten bread: **Now we hunger for your kingdom.**
We have tasted wine: **Now we thirst for your right.**
We have been asleep: **But now we are awake.**
We will meet you, Lord, whatever the time, the place, the cost:
We will come out to greet you. We will be there.

(423) *Christmas/Pentecost*

Living God, your promise is alive in all people,
however shadowed or obscured;
gathering those who are scattered,
giving bread to the hungry,
providing mercy for the poor.
For the Lord has saved his people:
He has filled us with good things.

Glorious God, your grace is at work throughout the world,
however fouled by malice or neglect;
mending those who are broken,
consoling the bereaved,
renewing the strength of the weary.
For the Lord has saved his people:
He has filled us with good things.

Peace-bearing God, your love desires joy for all humanity,
the satisfaction of plenty, gratefully received,
the security of abundance, honestly shared,
the offering of ourselves, generously given,
the blessing of a fulfilment in which all are honoured.
For the Lord has saved his people:
He has filled us with good things.

(424) *Christmas*

Giver of treasures, maker of relationships,
bringer of joy to celebrations –
you invite us to your table to find forgiveness,
peace, hope and love.
Build bridges of love between worlds and peoples.
Change meaningless toil into labour that heals.
May we know you in the grace of receiving.

(425) *Epiphany*

Loving God, as we follow your light
to the place of your revealing –
open our eyes to the needs of those who sacrifice is unseen.
Open our ears to the cry of those whose grief is unheard,
and be present with us as your star of hope
as we journey together towards that festival of your justice
which ingathers all humanity.

(426) *Covenant*

God of grace, we have pledged our faith to you
in word and deed, in prayer and aspiration:
Receive our love.
God of grace, you have pledged yourself to us
in the body of your Son, stretched out upon the cross,
in broken bread and outpoured wine:
Hold us in your peace.

(427) *Vocation/Unity*

O God our companion,
may we live together as those who have broken bread with you;
as a people who share truth and freedom and hope.
May we live together as those who have seen your dawning;
and who are alive, by your grace, to share your healing gospel
throughout the earth.

(428) *Vocation/Easter*

Traveller Christ, break the bread for us;
    reveal to us the mystery of your life of grace.
Pilgrim Christ, share the bread with us;
    tell us the story of your way through death to life.
Journeying Christ, pour the wine for us;
    sing us a song of love which is stronger than our pain.
Wayfarer Christ, walk the road with us;
    Stay with us on the path into right and justice and joy.

(429) *Lent/Holy Week*

Loving Jesus, living bread:
where human lives are abused,
sullied in mind, body or spirit,
there is your body broken.

Where there is famine,
and no bread for sharing,
there is your body broken.

Where families are split apart,
and bonds of love are severed,
there is your body broken.

Where there is plenty,
and bread is made only to be wasted,
there is your body broken.
Silence.

Lord, take the fragments of our hopes and fears,
bless them with your love,
and use them to feed the many hungers of the world.

(430) *Lent/Holy Week*

For that purity of heart and that singleness of mind
which looks for your sovereignty in our midst:
We pray to you, creative God.
For that humility which urges us to serve others before ourselves,
and to trust you for our daily strength:
We pray to you, generous God.
For that ardent devotion which perseveres in goodness, and upholds
the cause of right:
We pray to you, persistent God.
For that faithfulness which honours your purposes and values all
your creation:
We pray to you, gracious God
For that gratitude which accepts that you love us to the uttermost
and wish to feed us here with your living bread:
We pray to you, nourishing God.
For that hunger of the soul which is content to draw on you, and
yearns to be absorbed in your praise:
We pray to you, joyous God.

(431) *Lent/Holy Week*

Lord Jesus,
in obedience you lived for us,
following God's command wherever it might lead.
In obedience you died for us,
choosing faithfulness, even to death on a cross.
As now we remember your obedient sacrifice,
give us the strength to be obedient too,
so that, like you, we may enter into life eternal.

(432) *Lent/Holy Week*

'This is my body given for you,' you said,
and the following day you did just that.
'This is my blood shed for you,' you said,
and the following day you did just that.
Thank you, Jesus, that your word is more than just words,
but is the Word of God:
true, creative, dependable, life-changing.
Help us to respond to that Word,
as we eat this bread and drink this wine.

(433) *Easter/Pentecost*

Generous God, you saw us in need and reached out to us.
On the cross your arms were stretched out
to draw even enemies into your love.
We hunger and thirst for truth,
for a love which satisfies,
for a grace which will fulfill our deepest needs.
Draw us into your own infinite desire,
that all our yearnings may be gathered, purified, shared,
for the feeding of your children, and the healing of the world,
this day and forever.

(434) *Easter/Pentecost*

Here, Jesus, are the symbols of your death for us,
pledges of your grace, images of your limitless forgiveness.
Time after time we come to remember that you gave yourself for
        us,
and each time you welcome us, and free us from our wrong doing.
In this communion we see once more the cost of your love for the
        world.
Draw us into the mystery of your forgiving love,
which takes and absorbs our pain, our hatred and our hurt,
and transforms it into the power of reconciling peace,
Fill us with your Spirit, bless us with your grace,
and transform us with your love.
We ask this in your name.

(435) *Pentecost*

Humble God, hidden in our serving
as yeast is hidden in the dough,
you call us into a new community of hope.
Release in us the riches of your grace,
that we may trust in your unlimited power
as we serve the lowest and the least.

Humble God, hidden in our serving,
gather with us those who have been scattered by the evils of the
    world,
that here in your house of hope
we may find room for the homeless and the exile,
the prisoner and the refugee,
the vulnerable, the helpless and the frail.

Humble God, hidden in our serving,
call to this your feast all who are without protection,
that we may learn from the despised ones of the world
the wonder of your feast.

(436) *Pentecost*

Lord Jesus, as your broken body is shared with us, your broken
people, may we become whole.
As your poured-out life is offered us, so may we offer ourselves to
others in love and service.
As we are united with you in love, may we be one with each other.

(437) *Harvest*

As we draw food from the soil, and strength from the land, nourish
us with your love, Bread of life.
As we draw comfort from our friendships and encouragement from
the church, nourish us with your truth, Bread of life.
As we draw healing from our worship and renewal from our praise,
nourish us with your grace, Bread of life.

(438)

Strengthen us for service, Lord.
    So feed us with this bread and wine,
        that we may be ready and able to do your will.

Strengthen us for service, Lord.
So fill us with your Spirit,
that we may be channels of your love and joy to those we meet.
Strengthen us for service, Lord.
So guide your people by your grace
that your kingdom may come on earth as it is in heaven.

(439)

Feed our hearts, Bread of God,
that we may draw on your life and be strengthened in faith.
Feed our minds, Bread of God,
that we may carry your peace for the encouragement of others.
Fill our souls, Wine of God,
that we may serve you in humble service and in joyous praise.
Fill our lives, Wine of God,
that we may be poured out in love for the renewal of creation.

(440)

Feed us, O Bread of God,
that we may feed those who are hungry
for bread, or word, or hope.
Fill us, O Wine of God,
that your joyous grace may flow through us
into the wounds of the world.

(441)

Bless us this day, O generous King, with the gift of your only Son,
Jesus Christ. That we may feed on him as our daily bread, and
quench our many thirsts by drinking the wine which is his blood. Be
present with us in the gathering of our community, that our worship
and your sacrifice may be to the glory of your name in each street
and house, in each heart and life. We humbly bring ourselves to your
table, and pray that you will feed us.

(442)

Look upon us lovingly, all-powerful God, as we drink the fruit of the
vine and eat the corn of the fields in memory of your son. May the
bread that is broken for us be a remembrance of the gift of Jesus' life,
and the wine that is taken be a remembrance of his life-blood flowing
us.

Appendix 3 – Other Festivals and Special Occasions

References given after the Presentation are to numbers of individual prayers, or to themes listed in the Index.

CHURCH ANNIVERSARY

Genesis 28.10–22 *or* II Chronicles 7.11–16; Psalm 84 *or* Psalm 122; Ephesians 2.19–22 *or* I Peter 2.1–5; Matthew 12.1–8 *or* John 4.19–26

COMPANIONS ON THE WAY

Presentation
Illustration: sandwiches for a picnic. Talk about the fun (and hazards) of shared meals during journeys, drawing on experience of holidays, church outings, etc. If companions are literally those with whom we 'break bread' how do we share with others in our church so that we help each other go forward in pilgrimage? What does it mean to build each other up in holiness, so that we worship together in Spirit and in truth? How do we feed and refresh each other so that we are all strengthened for the journey? Can we draw strength for mission from our unity and common purpose with other Christians? Is our church a community which has discovered the gate of heaven, and so turns dry land into a 'place of springs' for others?

Call to Worship: 89
Adoration: 203 *or* 283
Confession: 284
Declaration of Forgiveness: 408 *or* 409
Thanksgiving: 205
Meditation: 286
Dedication: 362
Communion: 427 *or* 428
Dismissal: 70, 267, or 288

(See *Bread; Companions; Communion; Travelling; Way*)

PRAY FOR THE PEACE OF JERUSALEM

Presentation
*Illustration: a doll's house. Invite the congregation to imagine a
'house of peace' in which all sorts of people feel at home. Discuss:
what might the furniture or decor be like? Would everyone have their
own room, or would they need to share? What sort of food would
everyone eat? What special spaces would be needed for quiet, play,
television, music, talk, work? Note down contrasting expectations
and differences of opinion. Then ask: what would have to happen for
such differences to be honoured? What qualities would the people
need to have if they were to continue living together in their house of
peace? What are the implications for our worship and service?*

Call to Worship: 59 *or* I Peter 2.4–5
Adoration: 3 *or* 359
Confession: 243
Declaration of Forgiveness: 418
Thanksgiving: 217
Meditation: 206
Dedication: 92
Communion: 423 *or* 429
Dismissal: 207

(See *Foundations; House; Justice; Peace; People of God;
Priesthood; Repentance; Sacrifice*)

COVENANT

Exodus 24.3–11 *or* Deuteronomy 29.10–15; Jeremiah 31.31–34 *or* Romans 12.1–12; John 15.1–10 *or* Mark 14.22–25

On the theme of Covenant see p. 26 as well as: Confession: 108; Declaration of Forgiveness: 407; Communion: 426. This and the following idea could be adapted for other services of dedication.

LIFEBLOOD OF CHRIST

Presentation
Illustration: blood donor certificates or a donor card. Describe and discuss the process of giving blood, drawing out the reasons why people donate blood and pledge organs from their body so that others may gain benefit from our physical life. Explain that in ancient Israel the 'life' of the creature was so closely associated with its blood that there were rules surrounding the spilling of blood. To be sprinkled with the blood of a sacrificial victim was to be touched by a life made holy, and therefore to be made holy ourselves. To drink the 'blood' of Christ is to draw his consecrated life into ourselves, so that we are fed, not just with his strength, but with his strength surrendered to God. How might this affect the choices we make as to how we 'offer life' to others?

Call to Worship: 8 *or* 106
Adoration: 101, 107 *or* 359
Confession: 223 *or* 360
Declaration of Forgiveness: 402
Thanksgiving: 103, 113 *or* 116
Meditation: 339 *or* 373
Petition: 109 *or* 226
Dedication: 88, 225 *or* 239
Communion: 432, 441 *or* 442
Dismissal: 105, 111 *or* 363

(See *Body; God forgives us; House; Humility; Kingdom; Renewal; Sacrifice*)

HARVEST THANKSGIVING

Genesis 8.15–22 *or* Deuteronomy 26.1–11 *or* Ruth 2.2–23; Psalm 65;
I Timothy 6.6–10 *or* Revelation 14.14–18; Matthew 6.25–33
or John 6.24–35

A FEAST OF GOOD THINGS

Presentation
*Illustration: favourite foods. List the 'favourite foods' of the
congregation to compose a menu for a Feast of Good Things. Then
consider what other 'ingredients' might be necessary so that we can
truly enjoy such a feast, e.g. conversation, music, good company,
entertainment, speeches, etc. Where do thanksgiving, justice and
inclusiveness come in our priorities? Are they essential ingredients
or optional extras? How can we so enjoy the feast God provides that
we are prepared for the Harvest of eternity?*

Call to Worship: 241 *or* 277
Adoration: 15, 90, 152, 222, 269 *or* 365
Confession: 153, 237, 274 *or* 337
Declaration of Forgiveness: 415 *or* 419
Thanksgiving: 283, 398 *or* 95 (amending response to **God has
   provided for us**)
Meditation: 87, 96 *or* 339
Petition: 97 *or* 129
Dedication: 45, 98, 250 *or* 287
Communion: 423, 430, 437 *or* 440
Dismissal: 99, 281, 352 *or* 353

(See *Bread; Feasting; Generosity; God feeds us; Gratitude; Hour;
Promise*)

JOHN AND CHARLES WESLEY

(For use on 24 May, or on the Sunday nearest to 24 May if it is not Pentecost)

Isaiah 12.1–6 *or* Isaiah 51.1–3, 7–11; Psalm 130; Romans 5.1–11 *or* II Peter 1.1–11; Mark 12.28–37 *or* Luke 10.1–12, 17–20

THE OPEN DOOR

Presentation
Illustration: pictures of doors, some of them open. Discuss the pictures. What can we see on this side of the door? How much can we see of what lies beyond the door? Draw out the fact that while we are standing on this side, our view through the door is limited (even more so if the door is shut!) How then does our view change as we go through it? In what ways might it give us a view that we have never seen before? Christ is the Door: through him we have access to a new identity, vision, strength and understanding. Describe how John and Charles Wesley walked through the 'Door' in May 1738; going from 'depths to heights' in a few days as they saw for themselves the extent of God's love for them in Christ.

Call to Worship: Psalms 130.5–7a *or* Isaiah 51.1–3
Adoration: 165, 203, 209 *or* 303
Confession: 73, 140 *or* 298
Declaration of Forgiveness: 415, 416 *or* 419
Thanksgiving: 154, 205 *or* 367
Meditation: 328
Petition: 168
Dedication: 193, 199 *or* 266
Communion: 125 *or* 421/422
Dismissal: 144, 276 *or* 369

(See *Glory; God's transforming power; Inheritance; Joy; Living waters; People of God; Rock; Spring*)

REMEMBRANCE

Isaiah 25.1–9 *or* Isaiah 52.7–1 *or* Micah 4.1–8; Psalm 9.9–20
or Psalm 46; Romans 8.31–35, 37–39 *or* Revelation 22.1–5:
Matthew 5.1–12 *or* Matthew 5.43–48 *or* John 15.9–17

RIVER OF HEALING

Presentation
*Illustration: maps, photographs or other items relating to a river.
Talk about our experience of rivers and compare and contrast this to
rivers in the Bible such as the Nile. Draw out the fact that large
rivers have small beginnings; that they carry life to remote regions
in water and fertile silt, transport for people and freight; and that
they are 'highroads' for exploration and renewal. Compare this with
our task of remembrance; can we see ourselves as being part of a
'river' of humanity who have lived and died sacrificially for peace?
Note that the peace is not always experienced by the generation
which makes the sacrifices, but is realized 'downstream'. What
sacrifices might we be called upon to make so that the barren lands
can flourish and those downstream can receive the river of healing?*

Call to Worship: Psalm 46.1–7, Isaiah 52.7–10 *or* Micah 4.1–2
Adoration: 152, 236 *or* 365
Confession: 153, 237, 320 *or* 384
Declaration of Forgiveness: 406 *or* 410
Thanksgiving: 122, 154 *or* 374
Meditation: 87
Petition: 232 *or* 392
Dedication: 287 *or* 323
Communion: 424, 425 *or* 431
Dismissal: 213, 381 *or* 395

(See *Creativity; Forgiveness; God heals us; God of the nations;
Good News; Living Waters; Peace; Remembering; Violence;
Wilderness*)

WAITING IN HOPE

Presentation
Illustration: bus tickets, appointment cards. Discuss situations in which we must wait until someone is available to attend to our needs. What is hard about waiting, e.g. inability to settle to anything else, anxiety, disappointment, speculation? What kind of qualities do we need if we are to pay attention to what is going on during this time? Draw out how easy it is for waiting time to become wasted time. Then go on to consider how we 'wait in hope' for God's kingdom, especially in the fact of injustice, oppression and violence. What qualities should we bring to this kind of waiting? How can we prevent this waiting becoming wasted time? How can we pay attention so that we can see signs of peace, and enable them to bear fruit?

Call to Worship: Psalm 9.9–10; Psalm 46.8–11 *or* Isaiah 25.9
Adoration: 152, 209 *or* 384
Confession 102, 344, 351 *or* 360
Declaration of Forgiveness: 401, 402 *or* 411
Thanksgiving: 17, 80 *or* 321
Meditation: 155
Petition: 97, 218 *or* 356
Dedication: 176, 293 *or* 386
Communion: 420, 430 *or* 435
Dismissal: 163 *or* 170

(See *Bearing Fruit; Courage; Endurance; God keeps faith with us; Hiddenness; Patience; Remembering; Seeing*)

WATCH NIGHT

Deuteronomy 8.1–20 *or* Ecclesiastes 3.1–15; Psalm 8 *or* Psalm 90;
Revelation 21.1–6a; Matthew 25.31–36 *or* Luke 12.13–21
or Luke 12.35–40

WATCHING THE CLOCK

Presentation

*Illustration: clocks and watches. How many different ways do we use
to note or measure the passing of time? Make a list of the ones which
are important to us in different contexts whether short (seconds –
when running 100 metres) or long (the 'seven ages of man' – or
woman?). Draw out the fact that being aware of these phases is
important in 'knowing where we are' in the world; and that we use
anniversaries and other dates to remember the past in the present.
How can we use our awareness of time to celebrate the grandeur of
God and so remain humble, rather than acting as though the world
is controlled by our power?*

Call to Worship: Psalm 90.1–2 *or* Revelation 21.1–4
Adoration: 3, 101, 269, 303
Confession: 4, 102, 314
Declaration of Forgiveness: 401, 406 *or* 412
Thanksgiving: 165, 192 *or* 326
Meditation: 2 *or* 191
Petition: 322
Dedication: 5, 110 *or* 176
Communion: 420, 422 *or* 438
Dismissal: 6, 111, 133 *or* 246

(See *Hour; Humility; Power; Riches; Seasons; Temptation; Time*)

Index of Themes

Communion; Feasting; Life) of
life 57, 116, 125, 437 (see
Christ; Life of transformation;
Renewal)
Breath of God, wind as image
of Spirit 142, 144, 196, 212, 229,
232, 233, 349, 373 (see Mystery;
Living waters; Spirit)
Bridges 424 (see Barriers;
Communication; Conflict;
Diversity; Love; Relationships)
Broken, scattered 102, 153, 160,
173, 179, 187, 297, 421, 423,
426, 427, 429, 435, 436, 442
(see Christ; Humility) Broken
bread, 426, 427, 428, 429 (see
Bread; Communion)
Building (see Foundation;
Growth; People of God; Rock;
Temple)

Called (see God calls us;
Vocation)
Celebration 161, 309, 311, 315,
331, 371, 424, 425 (see Good
news; Joy; Worship)
Change (see God's transforming
power; Growth; Life of
transformation)
Children 10, 11, 36, 48, 185,
339 of God (see Inheritance;
People of God)
Choices 85, 88, 114 (see
Discipleship)
Christ 385, 412, 428, 434, 441
(see Body; Communion; Grace
of God) as Head of the Church,
399 (see Inheritance; People of
God; Riches) as intercessor 226,
305, 345, 371, 397 (see Prayer;
Sacrifice) as Saviour 113, 203,
219, 226, 237, 238, 249, 294,
297, 347, 391, 397, 399 (see God
our Deliverer)

feeds us, heals us (see Bread;
God feeds us; God heals us;
Grace; Shepherd) his
dedication, discipline, holiness
10, 149, 237, 239, 249, 345, 402,
431 (see Cross; Dedication;
Discipleship; Discipline;
Holiness) his humility,
vulnerability 10, 54, 64, 72, 78,
109, 148, 149, 160, 162, 166,
227, 328, 340, 347 (see
Humility; Love of God)
his suffering and death 51, 72,
166, 173, 175, 197, 199, 219,
223, 236, 238, 343, 397, 421,
431, 442 (see Cross; Death; God
suffers with us; Shepherd) risen,
ascended, alive 182, 185, 187,
188, 189, 190, 192, 193, 218,
219, 220, 236, 238, 303, 399
(see Dawn; Life; New birth;
Renewal; Resurrection)
Church (see Companionship;
People of God; Inheritance;
Love; Temple; Unity)
Christian unity (see
Communion; Companionship;
Diversity; God gathers us;
Reconciliation; Unity)
Cleansing, purification (see
Discipline; Holiness; Living
waters; Renewal; Repentance)
Colour, rainbow 2, 285, 309,
315 (see Beauty; Creation;
Creativity; Diversity; Unity)
Commitment (see Covenant;
God keeps faith with us; Keeping
faith with God)
Communication (see God hears
us; Humility; Love; Service)
Communion 101, 117, 125, 159,
160, 169, 259, 303, 328, 434,
436 (see Bread; Feasting; God
feeds us; God gathers us; Unity)

Community (see *Companion-ship; God gathers us; Feeding others; Love; People of God*)

Companionship, community 48, 50, 52, 60, 62, 64, 67, 79, 90, 106, 113, 159, 161, 190, 223, 229, 233, 238, 253, 255, 262, 267, 273, 278, 286, 299, 309, 310, 311, 316, 333, 338, 344, 357, 400, 406, 408, 427, 435, 441 (see *Love; Service; Travelling*)

Compassion 90, 103, 190, 192, 197, 207, 227, 231, 236, 242, 246, 259, 269, 292, 299, 310, 332, 335, 338, 343, 345, 352, 379, 380, 389, 392, 395, 399, 408, 412, 419 (see *Love; Need; Neighbour; Outcast; Service*)

Conflict, adversity, confusion, difficulty, harassment, suffering 107, 111, 130, 150, 162, 213, 230, 233, 262, 264, 266, 269, 295, 297, 321, 322, 324, 328, 352, 356, 374, 379 (see *Christ; Courage; Diversity; Endurance; Enemies; God suffers with us; Hatred; Oppression; Outcasts; Pain; Peace; Reconciliation; Violence*)

Courage, daring 150, 173, 316, 357, 368, 379, 380, 389, 392, 394, 418, 420 (see *Conflict; Enemies; God guides us; Into the Unknown; Risk*)

Corruption 384 (see *Discipline; Holiness; Seeing; Sin*)

Covenant 154, 176, 259 (see *Dedication; God keeps faith with us; Keeping faith with God; People of God*)

Creation 15, 90, 237, 241, 269, 274, 278, 283, 290, 350, 353, 362, 430, 439 (see *Creativity; Garden; Harvest; Pain; World*)

Creativity of God 42, 142, 153, 178, 212, 215, 233, 241, 262, 269, 303, 350, 430, 432 (see *Creation; Diversity; Feasting; Majesty*)

Cross 56, 109, 154, 156, 166, 236, 239, 266, 269, 323, 328, 333, 373, 426, 433 (see *Christ; Discipleship; Sacrifice*)

Cup, poured out. 291, 328, 391 (see *Blood; Life; River; Wine*)

Dance 189, 193, 198, 325 (see *Dawn; Joy; Singing*)

Danger (see *Courage; God guides us; Temptation*)

Dawn, new day, new beginnings, new song 1, 2, 3, 4, 31, 42, 49, 62, 95, 133, 176, 180, 205, 210, 241, 244, 252, 282, 287, 292, 293, 315, 325, 349, 359, 377, 381, 406, 422, 427 (see *God is doing a new thing; New birth; Renewal; Singing; Spirit*)

Death 129, 141, 143, 160, 162, 165, 168, 169, 172, 173, 175, 178, 179, 185, 192, 205, 264, 269, 285, 321, 361, 412, 414, 428 (see *Christ; Cross; Grief; Heaven; Life*)

Debts (see *Forgiveness; Sacrifice; Sin; Temptation*)

Deceit 73, 81, 91, 97, 117, 332, 350, 351, 378, 380, 381, 384, 414 (see *Holiness; Sin*)

Dedication, desire, devotion, dream 8, 75, 77, 84, 88, 92, 110, 149, 175, 192, 209, 218, 225, 256, 266, 276, 280, 283, 288, 303, 306, 333, 339, 355, 360, 368, 373, 383, 386, 423, 426, 430, 433 (see *Christ;*

guides us; Risk; Safety)

Feasting, plenty, abundance 41, 43, 44, 46, 50, 99, 101, 107, 152, 159, 161, 222, 236, 291, 340, 355, 361, 362, 365, 368, 373, 377, 383, 421, 423, 425, 429, 435 (see *Bread; Celebration; God feeds us; God gathers us; Gratitude; Harvest; Inheritance; Kingdom; Majesty; Table; Wine*)

Feeding, healing, liberating, refreshing, sharing with others, serving others 45, 123, 206, 207, 281, 287, 299, 310, 318, 320, 322, 326, 375, 386, 429, 440 (see *Freedom; Love; Neighbours; Renewal; Sacrifice; Service*)

Fire 101, 142, 193, 194, 229, 230, 249, 266, 320, 392 (see *Holiness; Spirit*)

Following Christ, footsteps (see *Christ; Discipleship; Walk; Way*)

Forebears in faith (see *Abraham; Inheritance; People of God*)

Forgiveness 152, 274, 327, 393, 406, 434 (see *Conflict; Dawn; Enemies; God forgives us; Hatred; Repentance*)

Foundation 128, 152, 153, 241, 242, 243, 359, 389 (see *God loves us; God our Deliverer; Obedience; Refuge; Rock; Standing firm*)

Freedom 44, 68, 116, 117, 118, 120, 192, 193, 197, 204, 212, 217, 225, 262, 267, 298, 303, 314, 326, 329, 332, 343, 350, 373, 376, 377, 384, 397, 405, 410, 434 (see *Boundaries; Discipline; God our Deliverer; Grace; Obedience; Life; Maturity; Renewal; Prisoners*)

Friendship 136, 141, 219, 238, 249, 255, 383, 397 (see *Covenant; God loves us; Love; People of God; Relationships*)

Fruit (see *Bearing fruit; Feasting; Fulfilment; Garden; Generosity; God feeds us; Harvest; Maturity; Spirit*)

Fulfilment of God's purposes 102, 104, 117, 146, 176, 178, 215, 218, 225, 236, 241, 245, 264, 278, 315, 334, 349, 350, 351, 360, 384, 402, 404, 423, 430 (see *also Christ; God's purposes revealed in Christ; Harvest; Hour; Kingdom; Majesty; Maturity*)

Garden, gardener, vineyard 45, 87, 155, 180, 222, 239, 279, 331, 351, 352, 353, 365, 398, 442 (see *Creation; God feeds us; God's transforming power; Harvest; House; Inheritance; People of God; Promises; Wilderness*)

Generosity 22, 38, 90, 92, 101, 105, 111, 128, 156, 160, 173, 174, 231, 242, 271, 277, 280, 284, 289, 291, 293, 297, 332, 334, 335, 337, 340, 341, 343, 374, 389, 390, 391, 394, 399, 419, 421, 430, 432, 433, 434, 441, 442 **of Christ** 149, 237, 238, 294, 297 **human** 223, 298, 311, 395 (see *Feasting; Grace*)

Gentleness (see *Christ; Love*)

Gifts, giving (see *Generosity; Feasting; God feeds us; Grace; Inheritance; Riches; Promises; Sacrifice; Spirit*)

Glory 13, 25, 60, 77, 101, 111, 120, 155, 168, 180, 187, 203, 215, 235, 313, 319, 362, 369,

228

205, 231, 238, 242, 262, 269, 277, 320, 337, 340, 349, 361, 371, 372, 373, 375, 381, 389, 423, 426, 427, 433, 434, 435, 437, 438, 440 (see *Forgiveness; God's transforming power; Life; Love; Mercy*)

enough, sufficient (see *Bread; Feasting*) **in action** 30, 81, 101, 222, 223, 237, 286, 289, 290, 327, 392, 418, 419 (see *Christ; God; Spirit*) **obstructed** 23, 173, 197, 230, 292, 310, 340 (see *Disobedience; Rebellion; Sin; Temptation*) **revealed** 60, 90, 107, 233, 286, 297, 357, 361 (see *Light; Seeing*)

revealed in us/others 29, 30, 56, 79, 92, 167, 223, 226, 227, 234, 239, 251, 284, 285, 295, 310, 318, 320, 327, 346, 361, 367, 394, 395 (see *Diversity; Feeding; Love; Neighbour; Outcasts; Service*) **revealed, shared through Jesus** 10, 22, 28, 29, 38, 48, 218, 219, 223, 226, 227, 231, 249, 273, 303, 310, 346, 409, 425 (see *Bread; Christ; God incarnate; God with us; Light; Shepherd*) **shared through the work of the Spirit** 229, 346, 408 (see *New birth; Spirit; Renewal*)

Gratitude 156, 218, 219, 264, 271, 281, 283, 375, 378, 386, 423, 430

Growth 87, 156, 176, 317, 340, 365, 366, 402 (see *Discipline; Garden; God teaches us; Maturity; Wisdom*)

Grief, mourning 170, 179, 180, 190, 193, 226, 245, 260, 262, 269, 379, 385, 399, 423 (see *Christ; Death; God; Pain*)

Guilt 108, 327 (see *Forgiveness; Repentance; Sin*)

Hands 18, 37, 96, 173, 176, 243, 269, 291, 320, 340, 361, 375, 380, 389, 393, 394, 397, 418 (see *Bearing; God comforts us*)

Harvest 129, 141, 332, 339 (see *Bearing fruit; Creation; Fulfilment; Garden; Hour; Judge; Seeds; Wilderness*)

Hatred 155, 165, 172, 216, 217, 269, 351, 362, 374, 390, 399, 414, 434 (see *Conflict; Enemies; Evil; Violence*)

Healing (see *Discipline; Feeding; Fulfilment; God heals us; Holiness; Maturity; Renewal*)

Hearts 88, 89, 113, 135, 138, 187, 222, 225, 226, 233, 256, 280, 303, 320, 338, 340, 341, 345, 350, 355, 360, 372, 373, 394, 398, 406, 439, 441 (see *Dedication; Holiness; Love; Renewal*)

Hearing (see *God hears us; Receiving; Seeing; Silence; Word*)

Heaven 84, 153, 385, 438 (see *Death; Fulfilment; Home; Hope; House; Life; Love; Maturity; Promises*)

Hiddenness of God 80, 97, 102, 154, 155, 270, 291, 294, 321, 392, 412, 425, 435 (see *Christ; Humility; Into the Unknown; Love; Mystery; Upside down God*) **of faith/sin** 110, 273, 295, 316, 327, 362, (see *Salt; Seeds; Yeast*)

Holiness, cleansing, purity of heart 35, 63, 64, 68, 71, 75, 79, 92, 107, 117, 162, 179, 192, 205, 217, 222, 225, 227, 229, 237,

439, 440 (see *Celebration;*
Dance; Dawn; God gathers us;
Singing; Wonder)
Judge, judgment 11, 109, 129,
135, 152, 160, 166, 172, 181,
217, 227, 362, 367, 398, 399
(see *Discipline; Diversity; Evil;*
Holiness; Hour; Justice;
Kingdom; Majesty)
Justice, injustice 68, 91, 102,
114, 169, 181, 185, 205, 215,
217, 220, 223, 229, 236, 293,
294, 298, 303, 310, 324, 333,
340, 358, 359, 363, 373, 383,
384, 398, 406, 418, 425, 428
(see *Love; Oppression; Outcasts*)

Keeping faith with God 57, 58,
75, 81, 85, 89, 92, 110, 121, 124,
128, 131, 169, 175, 218, 225,
232, 233, 252, 294, 346, 360,
368, 383, 386, 399, 407, 426,
430, 439 (see *Dedication;*
Discipleship; God keeps faith
with us; Hope; Love; Risk;
Trust)
Kingdom of God 11, 12, 16, 18,
81, 113, 199, 216, 217, 275, 288,
292, 366, 368, 389, 421, 422,
438 (see *Feasting; Fulfilment;*
God of the nations; Hour;
Majesty; World)

Life 85, 114, 116, 125, 141, 154,
172, 178, 180, 181, 189, 190,
209, 212, 225, 264, 269, 273,
290, 292, 315, 320, 321, 323,
337, 338, 339, 345, 352, 355,
361, 367, 372, 389, 391, 399,
402, 410, 412, 415, 428, 431,
436, 439 (see *Bread; Creation;*
Dawn; Grace; Growth; Living
waters; New birth; Renewal;
Resurrection; Spirit)

Life of transformation 56, 79,
140, 142, 143, 176, 179, 187,
199, 205, 210, 211, 243, 264,
266, 283, 292, 293, 306, 307,
314, 321, 347, 365, 414, 428,
432 (*Christ; Discipleship; God is*
doing a new thing; God's
transforming power;
Repentance; Sacrifice)
Light 1, 5, 6, 25, 28, 30, 41, 42,
52, 68, 133, 156, 168, 169, 203,
215, 349, 362, 372, 373, 377,
384, 390, 400, 406, 416, 425
Living waters 44, 87, 97, 152,
172, 179, 231, 232, 374, 398
(see *God refreshes us; Grace;*
Life of transformation; River;
Spirit; Spring)
Loneliness 62, 166, 169, 286,
288, 291, 399 (see *Alienation;*
Love; Reconciliation;
Relationships)
Love 16, 61, 73, 87, 92, 114,
159, 169, 232, 233, 275, 276,
283, 297, 304, 311, 316 (see
Neighbour; Relationships;
Service) **lack of** 91, 179, 230,
237, 274, 284, 292, 298, 311,
344, 350, 378 (see *Alienation;*
Loneliness; Sin) **our love for**
God 365, 366, 367, 382, 383,
426 (see *Dedication;*
Inheritance; Idolatry; Keeping
faith with God; People of God)
Love of God 90, 108, 136, 152,
192, 225, 229, 239, 241, 313,
317, 332, 349, 352, 355, 369,
373, 387, 405 (see *Covenant;*
God) **infinite, eternal** 67, 107,
152, 176, 179, 209, 265, 272,
273, 327, 333, 335 (see *God*
keeps faith with us; Into the
Unknown; Majesty; Mystery;
Time; Travelling; Way) **in**

action, at work through us 218, 222, 139, 293, 307, 317, 318, 326, 333, 334, 372, 374, 379, 391, 412 (see *Cross; Grace; Life of transformation; Love; Neighbour; Outcasts; Sacrifice; Service*) **gentle, tender, vulnerable** 78, 134, 172, 186, 242, 260, 271, 273, 279, 322, 380, 396 (see *Christ; Hiddenness; Humility*) **stronger than death** 178, 264, 385, 414 (see *Christ; Life; Life of transformation; Resurrection*)

Maturity, fruition, fulfilment, well-being, wholeness 209, 217, 237, 320, 321, 374, 402, 429, 436 (see *Bearing fruit; Discipleship; Fulfilment of God's purposes; God heals us; Holiness; Hour; Time*)

Majesty, kingship, reign, rule, splendour, sovereignty, of God 48, 101, 146, 215, 220, 222, 227, 236, 264, 293, 314, 322, 324, 331, 332, 338, 349, 355, 358, 359, 369, 371, 373, 381, 384, 390, 392, 396, 397, 399, 401, 420, 430, 441 (see *Glory; God of the nations; God's transforming power; Humility; Kingdom; World*)

Marvels, miracles, wonders of God 27, 48, 54, 180, 215, 297, 319, 331, 359, 380, 392 (see *God's transforming power; Grace; Mystery; Wonder*)

Mercy 97, 174, 176, 178, 184, 192, 217, 220, 223, 236, 237, 269, 284, 292, 297, 310, 312, 326, 327, 337, 338, 340, 351, 378, 382, 389, 390, 392, 393, 399 (see *Forgiveness; God forgives us; Love; Reconciliation*)

Mind of Christ, of God 77, 78, 383 (see *Hearts; Inheritance; Image; Love; Spirit*)

Mockery, contempt, cynicism, indifference, reproach 155, 175, 356, 362, 389, 393 (see *Cross; Rebellion; Spirit*)

Moses 128, 359, 362 (see *People of God*)

Mountain 103, 104, 152, 239, 359, 373 (see *Hiddenness; Mystery; Rock; Wonder; Word; Worship*)

Mystery 44, 48, 49, 66, 80, 101, 103, 104, 114, 154, 155, 166, 168, 174, 180, 190, 209, 210, 211, 222, 235, 297, 301, 315, 321, 362, 369, 371, 386, 412, 428, 434 (see *Hiddenness; Into the Unknown; Marvels*)

Name 209, 233, 249, 268, 309, 372, 380, 405, 434, 441 (see *God's transforming power; Inheritance; People of God*)

Need, humanity, vulnerability, want 209, 226, 250, 269, 291, 292, 298, 300, 304, 327, 340, 359, 367, 377, 383, 396, 405, 419, 425, 429, 433 (see *God feeds us; Neighbour; Outcasts; Pain; Service; World*)

Neighbour 91, 350, 366, 389, 399 (see *Companionship; Love; Need; Outcasts; Relationships; Service; World*)

New birth, born again, new life 121, 205, 315, 329, 402 (see *Celebration; Dawn; God is doing a new thing; God's transforming power; Life; Renewal; Spirit*)

314, 320, 329, 345, 351, 353, 373, 392, 399, 402, 414 (see *Broken; Death; Glory; God; Grace; Life; Life of transformation; New birth; Receiving; Rest; Resurrection; Spirit*) **of whole personality** 18, 260, 273, 320, 366 (see *Body; God heals us; Hands; Hearts; Maturity; Mind; Spirit*) **through repentance** 9, 107, 121, 143, 153, 197, 249, 350 (see *Repentance*)

Repentance, turning back to God 92, 222, 232, 249, 279, 290, 291, 315, 327, 337, 407 (see *Covenant; Forgiveness; Honesty; Humility; Renewal*)

Rest, recreation 132, 199, 211, 236, 258, 262, 299, 315, 344, 361, 372, 399 (see *Creation; Creativity; God heals us; Grace; Renewal; Silence*)

Resurrection 140, 141, 185, 186, 187, 189, 192, 323, 328, 385, 399 (see *Christ; Dawn; God is doing a new thing; New birth; Renewal*)

Reward (see *Inheritance; Heaven; Maturity; Riches*)

Riches, resources in God, wealth, 73, 122, 219, 230, 236, 278, 390, 435 (see *Bread; God feeds us; Inheritance; Poverty; Power; Promises; Seeds; Treasure*)

Risk 22, 317, 391, 392, 394 (see *Courage; God guides us; God our Deliverer; Refuge; Safety; Traveller*)

River, flow, life poured out, stream, tide 152, 337, 365, 384, 426, 428, 436, 439 (see *Blood; Cup; Living waters; Spring*)

Rock, stones, living stones 59, 202, 204, 206, 207, 283, 286, 288, 362 (see *Foundation; Garden; God guides us; Refuge; Standing firm; Temple*)

Room for all (see *God gathers us; Home; House*)

Sacrifice, cost offering 56, 76, 88, 92, 98, 116, 130, 143, 149, 155, 156, 157, 160, 162, 166, 167, 175, 197, 207, 223, 225, 227, 237, 238, 239, 275, 280, 286, 294, 298, 300, 301, 306, 310, 317, 324, 328, 333, 338, 339, 340, 349, 355, 359, 363, 368, 371, 373, 374, 386, 389, 422, 423, 425, 431, 434, 436, 441 (see *also Broken; Christ; Courage; Cross; Dedication; Risk*)

Safety 128, 140, 147, 199, 200, 204, 209, 338, 374, 377, 389 (see *Boundaries; God guides us; God our Deliverer; Refuge; Risk*) **false safety** 42, 153, 311, 316, 317, 322, 328, 389, 390, 392 (see *Barrier; Deceit; Idolatry; Power; Temptation*)

Saints (see *Companionship; Communion; Inheritance; Intercession; Love; People of God; Witness*)

Salt of the earth 79, 80, 82, 400, 416 (see *God's transforming power; Humility; Light; People of God; Seeds; Treasure*)

Saviour (see *Bearing; Christ; Cross; God our Deliverer; Refuge; Sin*)

Searching, seeking truth (see *Broken; God teaches us; Seeds; Seeing; Shepherd; Spirit; Receiving; Repentance; Truth;*

Vine, vineyard (see *Blood; Body; Cup; Feasting; Garden; Growth; Harvest; Inheritance; Judge; Life of transformation; People of God; Wine*)

Violence, war 79, 102, 169, 172, 179, 185, 216, 217, 305, 414 (see *Conflict; Cross; Death; Enemy; Evil; Forgiveness; Grief; Hatred; Peace; Reconciliation; Sacrifice; Stranger*)

Waiting 17, 23, 102, 155, 163, 170, 176, 209, 218, 291, 293, 323, 344, 351, 356, 360, 383, 384, 386, 389, 420 (see *God keeps faith with us; Keeping faith with God; Hope; Patience; Readiness; Silence*)

Walk 5, 84, 156, 190, 193, 239, 253, 257, 267, 290, 352, 409, 428 (see *Travelling; Way*)

Waste, abuse of Creation 153, 155, 167 (see *Beauty; Creation; God as Creator; Garden; Wilderness*)

Way, path, road 14, 15, 30, 52, 56, 67, 69, 84, 110, 113, 150, 154, 168, 190, 193, 194, 205, 237, 239, 257, 266, 283, 286, 299, 307, 323, 327, 333, 348, 351, 352, 361, 362, 379, 380, 381, 383, 389, 408, 409, 428 (see *Companionship; Discipleship; Preparing; Travelling; Walk*)

Weariness 147, 169, 179, 250, 253, 390, 423 (see *Bread; Endurance; God; Grace; Refreshment; Renewal; Spring*)

Weeds (see *Garden; Growth; Harvest; Seeds; Wilderness*)

Weep 218, 419 (see *Grief; Pain*)

Wholeness (see *Fulfilment; God heals us; God's purposes revealed in Christ; Holiness; Hour; Kingdom; Maturity*)

Wilderness, desert, desolation 117, 155, 175, 222, 229, 285, 286, 288, 297, 315, 341, 351, 352, 361, 377, 398 (see *Garden; God; Living waters; Preparing; Rock; Spring; Way*)

Wine 125, 422, 426, 432, 438, 439, 440, 441, 442 (see *Bearing fruit; Blood; Cup; Communion; Feasting; Garden; Harvest; Life; Sacrifice*)

Wisdom of God 42, 44, 73, 74, 76, 97, 98, 104, 212, 215, 249, 295, 313, 338, 349, 359, 362, 373, 384, 389, 390, 393, 399, 418 (see *God teaches us; Light; Seeing; Spirit; Truth*)

Witness, witnessing, witnesses, 20, 48, 57, 61, 62, 104, 105, 187, 188, 219, 220, 223, 226, 237, 386, 399 (see *God commissions us; Love; People of God; Service; Word; World*)

Wonder, adoration 22, 34, 222, 278, 365, 371, 383 (see *Glory; Majesty; Marvels; Mystery; Praise; Worship*)

Word 10, 42, 77, 93, 168, 196, 209, 250, 256, 283, 349, 350, 355, 361, 362, 365, 389, 397, 432, 440 (see *Bread; Christ; God teaches us; Spirit; Truth; Wisdom*)

Work 125, 262, 278, 280, 293, 305, 318, 327, 338, 389, 390, 418, 424 (see *Creation; Creativity; Grace; Love; Neighbour; Service; Witness; World*)

World 225, 226, 274, 283, 291, 294, 297, 300, 312, 338, 340,